TEX PERKINS

Tex Perkins has fronted some   ... ...tense
and spirited rock'n'roll bands – The Cruel Sea, The Beasts
Of Bourbon, Tex, Don & Charlie, The Dark Horses, Thug,
The Ladyboyz – and many other projects, including performing the music of Johnny Cash in the acclaimed Man In Black
theatre show. His take-no-prisoners approach to performance
comes with the sensibility of an artist committed to the subtle
(and often unsubtle) nuances of his craft. Throw in an astonishing voice full of power and depth, mix it with a dry and
sardonic sense of humour and what emerges is the reason there
is only one Tex Perkins.

STUART COUPE

Stuart Coupe (born 1956) has worked as a journalist, author,
editor, manager, record label director, radio presenter, publicist
and tour promoter. Career highlights include being the only
Australian to interview Bob Dylan twice, working with The
Clash, managing Paul Kelly and the Hoodoo Gurus and being
awarded a Ned Kelly Lifetime Achievement award for his contributions to crime fiction. He has written, co-written or edited
ten books, the most recent being *Gudinski: The Godfather Of
Australian Rock'n'Roll*, a biography of Australian music icon
Michael Gudinski.

Stuart currently presents weekly radio shows on Sydney
stations FBi and 2SER and works as a publicist for independent
Australian artists. He likes talking about Bruce Springsteen,
Bob Dylan and the Sydney Swans, not necessarily in that order.

TEX

By TEX PERKINS

with STUART COUPE

MACMILLAN
Pan Macmillan Australia

First published 2017 in Macmillan by Pan Macmillan Australia Pty Ltd
1 Market Street, Sydney, New South Wales, Australia, 2000

Reprinted 2017, 2018

Cataloguing-in-Publication entry is available
from the National Library of Australia
http://catalogue.nla.gov.au

Typeset in 12/18 pt Minion by Midland Typesetters, Australia
Printed by McPherson's Printing Group

Internal design: Alissa Dinallo.

Photo inside front cover, second row from bottom, middle photograph: courtesy of Mel McNamara.
Photo inside back cover, second row from top, second photograph from right: courtesy of Russell Kilbey.
All other inside cover images courtesy of Tony Mott and Tex Perkins.
Photos on pages 2, 155, 273, 281, 293, 298 and 309 courtesy of Kristyna.
Album cover on page 5 courtesy of Spooky Records.
Photos on pages 69, 75, 78 and 88 by Tom Takacs.
Photo on page 83 courtesy of Alain Rodier.
Album covers on pages 84, 107, 108, 119, 120, 121, 122, 123, 141, 142, 156, 157, 168, 176, 185, 186, 187, 188, 228, 232, 244, 245, 265, 275, 282 & 283 licensed courtesy of Universal Music Australia Pty Limited.
Photos on pages 91, 97, 98, 131, 139, 144, 159, 169, 180, 181, 195, 222, 227, 233, 300 and 303 courtesy of Tony Mott.
Photos on pages 94, 101, 103, 106 and 117 courtesy of Russell Kilbey.
Album artwork on pages 107, 108, 120, 121 and 123 by Tex Perkins.
Album artwork on page 120 by Ewan Cameron.
Photo on page 171 by Sophie Howarth.
Album cover on page 256 reproduced courtesy of BMG AM Pty Limited.
Album cover on page 284 reproduced courtesy of Level Two Music / Beautiful Kate Productions.
Album cover on page 308 reproduced courtesy of Liberation Music / Universal Music Australia Pty Limited.
All other photos courtesy of Tex Perkins.

To my beautiful children. Stop reading right now.

Seriously.

(Mum, you've already read too much.)

CONTENTS

DISCOGRAPHY

JUST LIKE ALTAMONT

'STOP THROWING BOTTLES AT THE BAND – THROW THEM AT MEEEE.'

Yes, here I was onstage at the Lava Lounge in Melbourne telling our audience to stop hurling bottles at the rest of the guys in the band. If they wanted a target, then aim for the frontman. And they did. And they hit me. Hard.

How had the Beasts of Bourbon disintegrated – or ascended – to this level of full-on confrontation with the audience? I asked for it.

This was probably the darkest, meanest, most in-your-face Beasts line-up. It was 1997. Rowland S. Howard, who supported us that night, wrote later that we were 'a lazy, insolent, cocksure, sneering, lascivious, threatening bunch of men.' He was right. Rowland also wrote that this gig was 'truly one of the greatest nights of my life' and that he later overheard a young girl breathlessly saying, 'It was just like Altamont!'

How had it come to this?

We had sound-checked and then gone to Chinatown to eat at a Japanese restaurant where we got on the saké – a special kind of drunk where anything can happen. By the time we got back to the venue we were pretty activated – me most of all. I'm bouncing off the walls before the first bands even start.

Rowland goes on first and it seems to me the audience aren't paying enough attention to him. He's playing solo and people are talking and ignoring him. This is Rowland Howard, you stupid fucks, ex-Boys Next Door and Birthday Party, one of the greats! I'm embarrassed and incredibly annoyed, pacing around watching from the side of the stage muttering to myself like an ice freak.

I decide there needs to be some more noise onstage to get the crowd to shut up. A drum kit is already set up for The Blackeyed Susans on next. I walk onstage and sit down behind it. Rowland says, 'And on the drums, ladies and gentleman, Tex Perkins.'

I start playing. I'm thinking I'm doing well. Not that I'm a drummer, but it's sounding all right. But nothing changes. The crowd are still looking uninterested. I storm off.

Next on, The Blackeyed Susans, now the crowd are into it? Dickheads. Shit-eating pricks! Fuck these shit stains! I'm furious. About to explode.

By the time the Beasts come on it's ugly. I'm sneering and taunting the audience. The crew are copping it, from the band AND the crowd. Microphones are getting bashed. Amps kicked over. We're all drunk, as usual, and we're playing . . . pretty well . . . but it's angry playing. *Fuck you playing.*

Pretty soon things start getting thrown. Rubbish and bottles are lobbing onto the stage. They're sort of aiming at the stage, and kinda at us. A few are lobbing dangerously close to Brian Henry Hooper, our bass player.

Brian is over it. He steps up to the mic. 'Throw whatever you like at him, but not at us.'

I grab the mic again. 'Yeah, they can't take it. DON'T THROW BOTTLES AT THE BAND – THROW THEM AT MEEEE.'

And then you could count it down. Three. Two. One. And from the back of the room this perfectly lobbed Crown Lager bottle sails maybe 30 or 40 feet, arcing through the air and cracking me in the middle of the forehead.

I've seen a photo of this moment and you've never witnessed so much childlike glee on the faces of the audience as

I'm hit. Just at the moment of contact they look so happy – totally entertained, like preschoolers watching a *Punch and Judy* puppet show.

Anyway, the hit is a beauty. My legs go wobbly. I buckle.

There's blood streaming down my face. I sink to my knees.

But then I decide that I want – I *need* – to keep playing. Partly it's blind rage, but mostly it's defiance. I can't let it end here. No, this has just begun.

I can literally taste blood on my lips now – the best kind, my own! We play more songs (after all I'm a professional). Blood is streaming down my chest – I'm that worked up and the room is so hot the claret pours out of me like a tap. I'm completely rabid! I start grabbing whatever I can find onstage and hurling it at the crowd. Plastic bottles, microphone stands, milk crates. Then monitors from the front of the stage. People scream, and run! It's complete madness – not so much of a meltdown as an eruption with more and more blood.

Security run onstage, tackle me to the ground and drag me off. The crowd are still baying like a pack of wolves chained to a lynch mob.

I give in to security pretty easily. I'm barely aware of what is happening. But I remember the curtains slowly closing. Bottles are still being thrown, a few getting through the ever smaller gap as the curtain closes.

I'm off to hospital for stitches. As I'm waiting at emergency, photographer Marty Williams turns up also needing medical attention. He'd been in the photo pit at the front of the stage and copped a few meant for me.

What had just happened left me totally exhilarated. I'm in a good mood, a very good mood, like I've just won a grand final or something. Instead of being consumed with anger or remorse I felt elated, and mischievous. Marty starts taking photos of me covered in blood, sneaking around inside one of the hospitals supply rooms. Another of me, limbs askew, posing on the hospital's waiting-room floor. A few years later it's the cover of the Beasts' live album *Low Life*.

When I look back on it today, I guess I did ask for it. I told the crowd to throw shit at me. And they did as I asked. Thank you. Now this wasn't the first time I'd had things thrown at me or the first gig where the audience were my adversary. But the one thing that sticks with me from that night, as I was staggering around the stage covered in blood, is I had this really strong sense that *this* – to be bleeding profusely, defiantly singing in front of a ferocious, ugly rock'n'roll band to an angry mob – was what I'd always wanted.

That *this* was what it was all about.

THE LIFE OF GREG

You probably know me as Tex, but I was born Gregory Stephen Perkins in Darwin on 28 December 1964.

But I will answer to Greg, Gregory, Perko, Mr Perkins, The Ape, Dad or Darling.

My dad's name was Robert Adolphous Perkins (aka Bob Adolph). Mum was Auriel Joan Anderson. All my brothers and sisters are a lot older than me and were born in different places. I was the only child born in Darwin. Before I came along there were two older sisters, then two brothers, then me. We were white, lower middle-class, Labor-voting Catholics.

The Perkins mob are Queenslanders. The family lineage comes from Thomas Perkins who settled near Toowoomba in 1864. He left England at the age of forty-two and came out here as a free settler, married an ex-convict Irish girl and there's been six generations since.

There was a period from the early to mid 1960s – maybe four or five years – when we all lived in Darwin. That's where the Perkins family first solidified. I don't remember it at all but the rest of the family look back at this time in Darwin fondly. This was Darwin between the times it was completely destroyed by the Japanese in World War 2 and then by Cyclone Tracey in 1974. I was about two when we moved to Brisbane in 1966.

Me and Mum, 1965.

Dad had been in the air force during the war serving in New Guinea, coming back to a public service job as an air flight officer. He started in air traffic control and worked his way into an administrative position. But he was always working at airports and that's why in the family's early life they moved around a fair bit. Longreach. Charleville. Cloncurry. All over Central Queensland.

In many ways, Dad was typical of fathers of that time. He left for work at 7.30 every morning and came home at six. He was the guy at the end of the table who got angry with me occasionally. He didn't cook or clean. He was as domestically uninvolved as most men of that generation were but he loved his lawn and kept it neat and mowed it regularly. Mum was the boss and ruled with skilful use of the Catholic mother guilt trip routine.

'Don't tell Mum,' was the code we lived by. We love our mum.

There was always music in our house. Nothing excessive, but it was there. A radio, a stereo, a piano or an uber-kitsch home family keyboard that Mum played a bit and that us kids could muck around on. So while there wasn't a great musicality in my family everyone listened to music and, probably more importantly, everyone had an opinion about music.

I always associate Dad with Marty Robbins, but Mum was into Perry Como, Val Doonican and those kinds of light crooners. My oldest sister Lyn was a bit of a hippie so she dug people like Bob Dylan, Donovan and Ravi Shankar. My other sister Beth was fairly mainstream in her tastes and listened to Marcia Hines and the like. My brother, John, was also kind of mainstream in his tastes and listened to things like Elton John. My tolerance for all that West Coast stuff like the Eagles and Fleetwood Mac comes from hearing him play his albums.

Looking back, I think my brothers had the most to do with my musical taste, especially my oldest brother Rob, who was into . . . well, rock'n'roll. He listened to the Modern Lovers, Iggy Pop, the Velvet Underground, the Sex Pistols and all that 'difficult' stuff, but also loved Jerry Lee Lewis, Gene Vincent and a very little known rockabilly cat called Ronnie Self.

Countdown was on every Sunday of course, and left a deep impression on me, but it was the radio that got to me first.

The subdued tones of late '60s Brisbane ABC breakfast radio transported my young mind to places like Richard Harris's 'MacArthur Park' and Glen Campbell's 'Galveston'. Donovan's 'Atlantis' told me of the destruction of an entire civilisation. Zager and Evans' 'In the Year 2525' forced me to consider the distant future of mankind. And Peter, Paul and Mary planted the seeds for a love of cannabis with 'Puff the Magic Dragon'.

It was Johnny Cash's 'A Boy Named Sue' that really got my attention. Apart from the vividly descriptive story of a bitter, violent man hell-bent on tracking down and killing his father for giving him a *girl's* name, more intriguingly it had words bleeped out! Words we weren't allowed to hear. Forbidden words. Words even worse than *mud* and *blood* and *beer*.

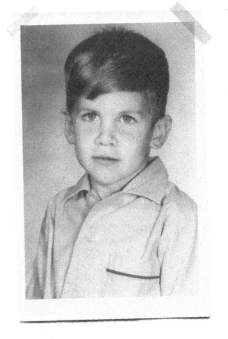

I can't remember having a genuine opinion about anything until the age of five. Of course I liked certain things and favoured certain flavours but I don't think it was until kindergarten that I thought of anything as good or bad. It was all just, there.

That's when I had my first win of any consequence – Best Dressed at the end of year (1969) fancy dress ball. Dressed as

Zorro – a hero of mine and easier to dress up as than my other hero at the time, Flipper – I wore an outfit made by Mum and beat other strong contenders such as the kid dressed as Fleegle from *The Banana Splits*. I definitely looked better on the arm of my co-winner, a little girl dressed as Cinderella than he would've. It was my inaugural triumph and an early example of my comfort wearing black.

A golden age of television was unfolding before me. Gerry Anderson kept me enthralled with *Fireball XL5*, *Stingray* and *Thunderbirds*. Saturday afternoon classics such as *The Ghost and Mr Chicken* and *The Reluctant Astronaut* starring Don Knotts were often replayed on TV along with the comic stylings of Dean Martin and Jerry Lewis and Abbot and Costello. And every afternoon at five o'clock we would drop whatever we were doing and come inside to watch *Lost in Space* and *Gilligan's Island*.

My very favourite television show was *Lancelot Link, Secret Chimp*, a 1960s show where all the characters were played by actual chimpanzees dressed up as people.

Lancelot Link was a chimpanzee secret agent – his boss was Commander Darwin at A.P.E. aka the Agency for the Prevention of Evil. It was a James Bond-style spoof show developed by the people behind *Get Smart*. I loved that show and I loved the album Lance made with his band, *The Evolution Revolution*. Someone recently told me that the chimp who played Lancelot is still alive and well, currently in his fifties and living the high life on the Wildlife Waystation in Southern California. *SHIT! He's my age!*

After my triumph as Zorro, the second significant accolade I remember getting was when I was in grade one or two. I'd drawn a picture of a monkey in a space suit and the teacher was so impressed I was taken to the principal's office where it was shown to him. It was one of the few times – the only one in fact – when I was taken to the principal's office for doing something right.

My next memorable accolade was for a school play where I played a monkey – a circus ape in fact. I was given a special award as 'the monkey who played the boy'.

Then, one Sunday night in the early '70s, my family gathered in the lounge room to watch the movie of the week: *Planet of the Apes*. I cannot overstate the effect this movie had on me. It blew my tiny mind. Apes with guns on horseback – it was the scariest, coolest thing I had ever seen. I loved the whole action fantasy thing of it, but like all great science fiction, it made me *think*, and introduced me to two huge concepts that resonate with me to this day.

Firstly, evolution. As a Catholic I had run into this theory early, but only in its debunking. 'I'd like to see the look on the face of the monkey that gave birth to a human!' said one of my first primary schoolteachers. But the idea that humans shared ancestry with not only apes but all creatures wasn't frightening for me. It was comforting.

And it didn't kill God for me, it *explained* God to me. It wasn't evolution OR intelligent design. If there was a 'creator' why couldn't they *create evolution*? I mean if you're a supreme being and you want to build a universe and all the things within it, surely you'd make systems that take care of themselves. You don't want to have to be there all the time puppeteering the whole thing, making sure everything's working and making adjustments when required. *You're a supreme being, you've got better things to do.* The main idea in *Planet of the Apes* is that evolution hasn't just stopped now that man rules the planet; it's ongoing. And in the absence of man's dominance, another

species will rise as his most fitting successor. Apes are the most likely candidate (but really it could be dolphins or pigs).

And why is man absent? Well, that brings me to the second mind-blowing concept introduced to me by this film: The Apocalypse! The idea that all this could end was heavy and it frightened, but also thrilled, me. A post-apocalyptic world was free of responsibilities – no school, no cops, no rules! Everything looked cool, all ruined, wrecked and rusted. You don't even have to wear clothes on the planet of the apes! No wonder Desmond Morris's book *The Naked Ape* later became my bible.

Just for being in this movie Charlton Heston became my favourite actor. I didn't realise at the time just how bad an actor he was because his movies – science fiction and religious epics like *Ben-Hur*, *El Cid*, *The Ten Commandments*, *The Omega Man* and *Solent Green* – had other things going for them.

But it was *Planet of the Apes* that owned my soul.

My interest in apes began early. My long arms and heavy brow led many to call me 'Monkey Boy' or 'The Ape'. Usually calling someone an ape is a derogatory thing but it's never bothered me. I love apes.

To embrace my inner ape was to connect with my true nature and ultimately it explained, even justified, my darker tendencies. Two sides to the one banana pancake.

I was a clown of a kid who was always trying to entertain in some way. Always seeking the joke, gag or a prank in whatever was going on. There was a family tradition where I would get in my father's overalls and stuff them full of pillows becoming this giant pillow-child busting moves on the front lawn so I could be seen by passing cars. I'd waddle around the yard pretending to trim the edges or something, trying to get a look on people's faces as they drove by.

When I was about eight, I was taken to the Brisbane show (the Ekka) and given a full-head gorilla mask which I wore all day. Never taking it off, drinking my Coke through a hole in the mouth with a straw, I jumped out at people, attempting to frighten them – not uncommon behaviour at the Ekka.

On the train ride home I changed my strategy. Rather than leaping out at people I would quietly sit near them and wait for them to glance up. Did this kind of behaviour lead to a career on the stage? I dunno, but I've always had a love of mischief and still seek it out and embrace it in any form.

For me it's not necessarily about being watched and being entertaining, but more about creating some sort of unexpected situation. Situationism is an art movement often using performance appearing in normal life rather than a stage. Sometimes a mixture of social experiment, performance art and pranking, it could involve almost anything. Throwing unusual elements into a public space, stepping back and seeing what happens sounds good to me. From Situationist to Entertainer is an easy step to make. I wanted to *make things happen*. Still do.

The Boondall Drive-In cinema was half a block from my house. This place was hugely important to me all the way through my childhood. From being taken there in my pyjamas aged five to see *Chitty Chitty Bang Bang* to sneaking under the fence with my mates aged ten to driving 'borrowed' cars and fooling around with girls aged fifteen.

The drive-in was an almost magical place to me. There I saw everything from *Jaws* to *Dawn of the Dead*. I first saw *Apocalypse Now and The Deer Hunter* at the drive-in.

The drive-in knew how to make an event out of the showing of movies. Even now I've still never seen anything like the double bill of *Mad Max* and *Stone*, both Australian-made and both attracting an audience just as scary as the characters in the films, with every bikie and rev head in the northern suburbs turning up. Interaction with the action on the screen came in the form of horn honking, the revving of hotted-up engines and the odd donut and burnout. Muffled screams and laughter emanated from inside a hundred panel vans.

Me and my mates took this all in from the kiosk, where we

scoffed Jaffas and plotted mischief. On another night myself and three other boys from the neighbourhood crawled through the hole in the fence under the big screen. We'd done this many times before when we wanted to sneak in to see a movie, but tonight was different. On this night we all stood in front of the screen swinging burning steel-wool pads tied to lengths of string. A waterfall of burning metal embers showered like a million sparks in front of the drive-in movie.

A hundred horns honked angrily at us from out of the darkness. But we kept right on swinging until the security guard chased us all the way to the fence, grappling at our feet as we made our escape. Now *that* was fun. Being chased by the security guard at the drive-in was a local sport all boys who grew up in Boondall took part in over the years.

When I come back to Brisbane these days to visit my mother I often drive past where the Boondall drive-in used to be. Just as many houses cram into the space where once cars did. You know those suburbs where the houses have the same coloured roofs and are one of only two standard designs? It's incredibly depressing to look at, but I still have waves of nostalgic feelings wash over me as I drive along that road. Good feelings.

Nothing bad ever happened to me at the drive-in.

Being Catholics we went to Mass every weekend and we all sang. Except me. I was convincing enough when I mouthed the words. As a young child I embraced church like most kids my age do. Then, inevitably, I started listening to what they were saying. Firstly I just got bored with it – there was a zoning-out period around the age of ten where I thought, *I wish I could be . . . anywhere else.*

Later on I really took in what I was hearing every Sunday, and started questioning it, suddenly aware of the hypocrisy that was everywhere around me – at school, at church – these unquestionable institutions started to seem . . . questionable.

Around this time, music, mostly words with melodies, started arriving in my head, like they were transmitted into me from an outside source. The first time I can remember this happening I was still in primary school and my mind was wandering.

In one town there's sundown
And in another town there's morning rise

This basic lyric rattled around in my noggin for weeks, for no reason at all. It wasn't part of a school project. I hadn't thought, 'I'm gonna write a song'. It just appeared. I told no one of course. It wasn't very good.

The next time I had occasion to exercise this skill was part of school work. Homework to be exact. The task was to write a poem in the classic style of the Australian bush balladeers. Henry Lawson and Banjo Paterson.

My own composition 'Wentworth Plains' was the story of a stubborn old prospector who, despite everyone's disbelief that Wentworth Plains would ever yield any gold, toiled away for years regardless. I can't remember how any of it went, but the last line describes his skeleton being found with a large gold nugget clutched in its bony fingers. I was pretty happy with and it and showed it to my father, who suggested a few small changes.

'Plagiarism!' cried Brother Shithead after reading it. 'You didn't write that! You've copied it from somewhere!' Brother Shithead couldn't pinpoint where I'd stolen my work from, but he told the class and his colleagues, 'That idiot Perkins couldn't have written this,' and graded me zero out of 10. This was despite the whole point of the exercise being to write 'in the style of'. Yes, yes, a sign of things to come.

As a kid I rode my bike everywhere and it opened the world up for me. I had independence and could be anywhere. For me that meant places other than where I said I'd be. I'd tell Mum that I was going to the 6 pm Mass, then I'd 'go down the bush' as we used to say. This was the area beyond the train line and had bike tracks weaving through to the creeks, swamps and mangroves. I'd ride my pushy through the bush with my slug gun for an hour, then head home and be there at the same time I'd arrive if I'd been to Mass.

In my childhood loner-years it was just me, my pushbike and my air rifle. It's amazing to think of that now. A 14-year-old riding around on a pushbike *with a gun*. That just couldn't happen these days, could it? But back then I'd ride into the bush and spend hours shooting cans, old cars and bits of tin. I shot a bird once and instantly felt the pointlessness of it. I never shot anything living ever again. But I have to admit, being a Queenslander I've killed many cane toads. Mainly with a golf club. It was my civic duty.

My first bike, a MALVERN STAR three-speed dragster (not the bike in the story, which was a one-speed with foot brakes and angel bars).

One time while cruising through these bush bike tracks near Cabbage Tree Creek with my two best friends (my bike and my gun) I came across what looked like an old washed-up (literally) dinghy. Well, that's what I told myself anyway. It was old and a bit shitty but there were no holes and it looked like it would float. Hmmm, a boy with his bike, gun and boat?

Nobody will miss it, I thought. I threw the bike and slug gun in the boat and began pushing it towards the water. I thought I'd take it up creek and stash it in some secret location of my choosing. As soon as I got into slightly deeper water I noticed it was crowded with jellyfish. I mean it was thick with the horrible things. More jellyfish than water. There were no oars so I used a bit of driftwood I'd found nearby to paddle and steer my new craft through these treacherous waters. I needed to head up the creek and luckily the tide was moving where I needed to go. So all I had to do was get out far enough and away I would float. I started drifting up creek which took me straight past all the fishing trawlers that worked in that part of Moreton Bay. As I was passing the last one, an angry voice broke the quiet.

'WHAT THE FUCK!? THAT'S MY DINGHY . . . HEY YOU LITTLE CAAARNT.'

A group of fishermen were having beers together on the back deck of the trawler at the end, and one of them was on his feet pointing and screaming at me. For a moment I think he considered diving in, swimming over and murdering me. But one look at the water chock-a-block full of jellies and he quickly reconsidered. So we just stared at each other as I floated past, just metres from each other. So near but so far. I reckon I'm lucky they didn't have a gun. More abuse from the other fishermen followed as I drifted off up the creek, shored the dinghy and escaped back into the bush on my bike.

When I was on the verge of turning 15, after a few years of going to the creek and not to Mass, I finally worked up the guts to say to Mum and Dad that I wasn't going to church anymore. I told them I just wasn't into it.

It was one of those situations where being the youngest had its advantages. I'd seen this conversation go down before with my brothers and knew there was a bit of flak coming after the initial delivery of the message, but that it was worth it in the end. I just had to go through it once and then I'd never have to go through it again. So that's what I did. Mum was disappointed and Dad was angry . . . for a minute. Then we all, very sensibly, moved on.

I retained some appreciation of spirituality from my time participating in religious activities, or at least it got me thinking. But even at 14, I knew that if there was a God it wasn't the one *they* were selling me. 'I'm not saying God doesn't exist, but I know that your god doesn't exist.'

There's a seven-year gap between myself and John, the next youngest, so the four others had this unity from having grown up together that I never felt. My sisters had moved out of home by the time I was nine or 10 so they weren't around. It was my brothers who had the most to do with the way I am – not only my tastes but my tendencies. I'm talking about not only things like sense of humour, mannerisms and accent, but also the dark stuff. My brothers were the first to nurture my hurt and hatred. Back then John enjoyed tormenting and torturing me. I had taken his place as the 'cute little guy' in the family, and he didn't think I was worthy. He hated what he thought I got away with.

I think Mum and Dad parented the first four kids with a harder old-school attitude. By the time I came along things were a bit more relaxed. The recurring thing I heard from John to Mum and Dad was: 'HOW CAN HE GET AWAY WITH THAT? I WAS NEVER ALLOWED TO . . . BLAH BLAH BLAH.'

I didn't really get away with much. Just little things. I got sent to a slightly more expensive school. Mum and Dad were older and maybe there was a little more money around. Perhaps John resented that life seemed easier for me than it was for him. But it's always like that – the eldest kids in a family pave the way for the youngest.

It's no secret my parents were hoping for a daughter when I was born, simply because daughters are a lot easier. Their experience with Lyn and Beth was a lot nicer and neater, they helped out more around the house. The Perkins boys were messy and violent and got into trouble.

My father wasn't a tough guy, but that era of men didn't know how to be affectionate. I remember that when I'd hug him he was always very stiff and would hold himself in a strange way. He would almost withdraw from it and it was always awkward. So I would almost force it on him – 'Give me a hug you old bastard' type of thing. It wasn't his fault. Dad was just a product of his time; those men weren't greatly affectionate. There were many moments when I sensed his disappointment in me but I think that softened as the years went by.

Dad.

WELCOME TO MY NIGHTMARE

Sometime in 1978 my father was once again transferred to another city because of his job.

This time, rather than uproot the family, he decided to go up to Townsville alone. And a few months later during the Christmas holidays my mother went up to visit him.

That meant leaving all us boys ALONE AT HOME. I was 13, my brother John was 19 and Rob was almost 21. Mum would be gone for a few weeks so it meant I would be all alone with my big brothers and they would be taking *really good care of me*.

Early one Saturday morning after Mum had left, my brother John came into my room and said, 'Get out of the fucking house today and don't you dare come back until 4 o'clock . . . or I'll kill you,' and handed me twenty dollars.

'NOW!!'

'Okay, okay, where will I go?'

'I DON'T FUCKING CARE DICKHEAD. JUST GO FAR AWAY AND DON'T COME BACK UNTIL 4 PM.'

I should point out, ladies and gentlemen, that twenty dollars was a lot of money to a 13-year-old in 1978. This was a good deal and I happily accepted the terms. FAR AWAY and 4 PM. Got it.

Within five minutes I was out the door and on my way to the bus stop. I would bus it down to Toombul Shopping Town and see what took my fancy.

Hmmm, first I'll buy a cream bun and an iced coffee from the bakery. That should set me back about 80 cents. Then I'll go to the newsagency and buy the new *MAD* magazine. That's another dollar fifty. Then I'll head on down to Toombul Music and . . . who knows?

Toombul Music sold stereos, musical instruments and records and cassettes. Don't get the wrong idea here. Just because they had all those things doesn't mean this was some groovy record store where the kids hang out and vibe on tunes. No, Toombul Music was not cool in any way. But this was the only music emporium I knew, and the place where I began to dream *rock dreams* – imaginings brought on by staring at and into a record cover.

I nearly bought Boston's *Don't Look Back* that day just for the front cover. Gerry Rafferty's *City To City* album was a consideration, it's got 'Baker Street' for fuck's sake! The *Grease* soundtrack? Narrrr. Wings' *London Town*? Hmmm . . .

Then my eyes fell upon it. *Welcome to My Nightmare* by Alice Cooper. This album had been out for a few years and was considered a modern classic. Only recently had it been replaced by Meat Loaf's *Bat Out of Hell* as the big-selling mainstream 'concept' album of the day.

But even then I didn't *get* the Loaf. Not much music makes me upset. His does.

So, perhaps based on his recent appearance on *The Muppet Show*, I went for Alice! And I've never regretted my decision. It cost $8.99 brand new and I still enjoy that album to this day. I'm not listening to the *same* actual album from that day of course. I would've lost/left that, somewhere sometime in the '80s. Even though I realised even then that this album actually marked the end of Alice's golden age – *School's Out, Billion Dollar Babies* and *Love It to Death* are better records, I love *Nightmare*. The title track is sleaze funk at its best, 'Only Women Bleed' is a twisted feminist anthem and if you can't quote every word of Vincent Price's 'Black Widow' monologue, you're just not a fan.

It was my entry into another world, and this time I was going in alone. Nobody else in my family would join me on my Alice journey. This was my decision. This was MY record bought with MY MONEY – money that I had earned by doing a good job of NOT being at home until after 4 pm!

I looked at the time; it was 11.30 am. Four-and-a-half hours to go. I killed another two hours reading my *MAD* magazine and eating a pie very slowly. By 2 pm, I was going crazy. I had about seven bucks left, and wanted to put it towards my next record purchase, probably Bowie's *CHANGESONEBOWIE*.

I don't know what possessed me, but at 3pm I decided I would call home and see if it was okay to come back a little earlier. The phone rang, and it rang for a while.

Suddenly, my brother's voice came on the line, 'Hello?'

'Hey, it's me, can I come back yet?'

In the background I could hear Rod Stewart's 'Da Ya Think I'm Sexy?' on the stereo.

'FUCK OFF,' came John's reply, and he slammed down the phone.

John must have been taking private dance lessons, I guess, so I decided to stay away for a little longer than 4 pm. When I came back closer to 5 pm, 'WHERE THE FUCK HAVE YOU BEEN?' was my greeting.

'HOW MUCH CHANGE HAVE YOU GOT FROM THAT TWENTY?'

'Seven bucks,' I proudly stated. What an idiot.

'GIVE IT HERE.'

'But . . .'

The remaining seven dollars was gone. But hey, I had Alice, and despite the lessons John never became a very good dancer.

SCHOOL'S OUT

High school was St Joseph's at Nudgee, one of those big thriving powerful Catholic schools full of rich graziers' sons, sent there as boarders.

Imagine that, living at school . . . it sends shivers down my spine, even today.

At the main entrance was a statue of St Joseph, with three small holes in the middle of its back. Saint Joe was set high on a pedestal so it was difficult to do a ballistic autopsy, but the legend was that some kid in the '50s came back to the school brandishing a gun, demanding one of the brothers come out and face justice. The brother wasn't silly enough to do that, so before the kid was dragged away by the cops, St Joseph copped it instead.

Whatever could have happened to that kid to make him want to do a thing like that?

Look, before I go any further perhaps I should tell you this little story. One lunch time the usual sounds of schoolground shouts and chatter were interrupted by a boy running through the quadrangle wearing only school swimming speedos shouting at the top of his voice, 'HE TOUCHED MY PENIS! HE TOUCHED MY PENIS!' A Brother, let's call him Brother Flannagen, had lured this lad into his living quarters for a 'private photo session'. Brother Flannagen then went around to each class and explained that, yes, he had touched the boy's penis, but was moving it 'for photographic purposes'. I think in the porn industry they call that a 'fluffer'.

My school years were a stressful period for me in general.

At about the age of 12, I'd had a massive growth spurt and seemingly overnight became freakishly tall and painfully skinny. A fact I was constantly reminded of by everyone from my grandmother to the football coach. I remember struggling with puberty on many levels. I had migraines and was extremely awkward. There was way too much going on in my head. Gradually my grades turned to shit.

There was a very controlled, systematic use of violence at Nudgee. Boys were struck with this thing called a 'gat' in a very orderly corporal punishment kind of way. The brothers called it a strap, but we called it a 'gat'. I don't know why. It was an inch thick, two-inch wide, foot-long chunk of hard black plastic specifically designed for hitting young boys on the hands and buttocks. It was standard issue. Every Catholic brother had one. Some of them decorated the 'gat' with small stickers of religious icons, some lovingly bound theirs in leather.

Those freaks were bad enough but nowhere near as bad as the free-form violence of the lay teachers. Where the brothers liked the ritualistic 'six of the best', the lay teachers included a number of psychopaths that at any moment could lose it and some kid would be grabbed by the hair and have their head beaten against the blackboard while the teacher screamed: 'WHY CAN'T YOU UNDERSTAND?!!?'

We had this tech-drawing teacher who was notorious. We'll call him Phil. He was probably in his mid-fifties, with a hair-trigger temper. A volcano ready to blow at any moment in the most unpredictable manner. I will never forget the day Phil was up at the blackboard, drawing something with chalk using his giant size T-square when someone dropped a pencil, moved a chair and bumped another kid's desk, who then made some small verbal utterance.

Without fully turning around and assessing the situation, Phil threw his giant T-square in the general direction of the disturbance. The T-square, not designed for flight, skimmed the heads of the first three rows then boomeranged upward and smashed through the large glass louvered windows, showering us all in broken glass.

The year after, Phil had a stroke, right there in front of a class. Unfortunately, I wasn't there to see it.

But you know what? He wasn't the worst of them.

I was on edge *all the time*. I couldn't think straight when I was wondering what form of violence was going to happen next and whether it was going to involve me. I was having enough trouble coping with being that age as it was without the threat of being physically assaulted if I didn't understand something – or dropped a pencil.

Then at the age of 15 a light bulb suddenly turned on in my head. I thought, *Wait a minute, this ain't right*, and the next time a teacher told me to put out my hand because they'd decided they needed to hurt me to educate me, I said: 'No, I'm not going to do that.'

I started questioning everything. They'd say, 'God gave His only son Jesus to the world so He could die on the cross.'

'Sir, why did Jesus have to die on the cross?'

'To free the world of sin.'

'Really? So how'd that turn out?'

Yes, I was a smartarse, but that came with my new state of mind. I could no longer take these people seriously after I'd realised, *You're not only wrong, you're evil*. From that moment I had a real sense that I was the calm, logical one in this situation. This became far more confusing and confronting to my teachers than if I'd been a wild child, screaming and throwing punches. I just looked at the teachers and said, 'I'm not allowing you to hurt me any longer.'

Once I wasn't afraid anymore, the teachers lost their power over me.

In the end the vocational officers and the teachers thought we all might be better off if I left school early. I had good results in Art and English and low scores in everything else. I was interested in music but the notion that I could be a musician or somehow work in the entertainment world was a fantasy everyone said you could never take seriously as an option.

Back then the vocational officers at the school would look at your report card, have a quick chat and suggest a career: 'Why not become a doctor?' or 'Your future is in finance . . . working the cash register at McDonald's.' It wasn't an issue with a lot of these kids as when school finished they were just going back to help run their dads' properties.

My father didn't expect me to follow him in any career sense, because there was no real tradition to continue on. He was a public servant working in a department at the airport.

It wasn't like he had a family business to pass on.

Me? I had Art and English. That's all I had a chance of kicking goals in. So what do they come up with for me as a career suggestion? Signwriting. They figured because it involved a paint brush and there's letters and words involved that's my go. After 10-and-a-bit years through the meat grinder of a Catholic boys' school education, this was where I'd been led.

The writing was on the wall.

And it was misspelt and messy.

GUITAR

I'd been given my first guitar Christmas Day 1978.

It was a cheap but functional acoustic. After fiddling and fumbling around with it for a month or two I decided I needed guitar lessons. I had grasped a couple of things. My brother Rob showed me how to do a two-fingered way of playing 'Stepping Stone' by The Monkees, and using the same technique I'd taught myself 'Smoke on the Water'. But proper guitar lessons were the obvious next step.

Music wasn't part of any school curriculum. No way. This place didn't even have a choir. So to get to lessons I had to leave school *then come back*. AT NIGHT. This was a huge deal. To actually go back to school for anything (other than vandalism) when you didn't have to was crazy. You had to *really* want to learn an instrument to do that.

But I took my acoustic guitar and went along for lessons. Catholic schools have a weird ominous vibe at the best of times, but at night, they are creepily silent.

My guitar teacher was this enormous man – he must have been six foot six. A really tall, old fella that hunched over his guitar with incredibly distorted bulbous knuckles and yellow nicotine stains on the inside of his fingers. His hands were these arthritic, alarmingly grotesque-looking monster mitts. These are the hands we had to look at as he wheezed his instructions and we followed his lead.

But he was grumpy and totally unenthusiastic about what he was there to do. This guy clearly didn't like teaching music and I suspect he didn't like hearing it either. He tried to show us stuff like 'Yellow Submarine' but the way he played it sounded nothing like 'Yellow Submarine' to me. He may have had the chords right but it was as if he'd never heard the song and had no instinct for melody whatsoever. It was ridiculous. I think I did three lessons with him and realised I had to walk away.

'Why did you quit guitar lessons, Greg?'

'Because I love music.'

I kept the acoustic guitar but I rarely enjoyed it. It was a real struggle. Still is.

My fingers hated it and I'm not an equipment kinda guy. To be a real guitar-strumming kind of fella you have to love your stuff, take that acoustic guitar out and polish it, even oil things, I think. I didn't even like changing strings.

A few years later I got myself an electric guitar and that's when things came alive. A one hundred dollar Audition brand in dark mahogany with a black scratchplate. With an electric guitar all I had to do was hit one string and let it ring and it sounded good. If I added reverb and/or distortion, well fuck me!

Chords came later. I actually don't think I played a chord until I was about 10 years into my musical career. I mean, I was a singer after all.

1980

Nineteen-eighty was a big year for me.

Not only did I quit school that year but I re-evaluated my whole personal aesthetic in regard to how I dressed and what music I listened to. For a 15-year-old those two things are extremely important and *intrinsically* linked.

I had been listening to rock'n'roll records of my choosing for a few years, but being a school kid, I'd never dressed the part. Or maybe I had. I mean what did a Led Zeppelin fan wear anyway? If it was a Golden breed t-shirt, flared jeans and a pair of thongs, then I had pretty much nailed it.

But mainly due to the access to and influence of my brother Rob's record collection, I was slowly TURNING PUNK.

It helped that some of the bands I'd been listening to during my early teens had been releasing pretty awful albums.

Led Zep's *In Through The Out Door* sounded soft and over-produced – a tired flabbier shadow of their epic former selves. And Kiss, who I'd loved just two years before, had put out what I still believe to be one of the worst records in the history of rock, *Unmasked*.

Just five years earlier, before the phenomenal success of their disco hits, Kiss were a band Brisbane kids knew very little about. There was a mystique about Kiss. They seemed weird and dangerous. *Bad kids* had Kiss albums – kids that got into trouble a lot, kids you'd find smoking behind the tennis sheds. We would pore over the album covers exchanging often bullshit information:

'See that blood coming out of Gene Simmons' mouth? That's just after he'd bitten the head off a white dove!'

'Really? Woah!'

'And he's had a cow's tongue transplant.'

'Faarrk.'

Kiss fans' loyalty had been tested with the previous album *Dynasty* but *Unmasked* – typified by the disgustingly awful dribble of the single 'Shandi' – was so bad that it tipped me over. I was out.

Pink Floyd still had me believing in the worth of classic rock with the magnificent torrent of bile that is *The Wall* but that was really the last hurrah from the old guard. Bands like Devo, the Dead Kennedys and the Ramones seemed a lot more fun.

I went to three big rock concerts in 1980: The Ramones, AC/DC and Kiss. Even though I had already written Kiss off and moved on, I couldn't help myself. I had to have one last look. And what I saw was four clowns with fireworks and a light show.

Worse, the concert at Lang Park in Brisbane wasn't full of bad kids, but LITTLE kids! Literally, mums and dads and their seven-year-old daughters. This was the last straw – it was monumentally lame.

I also went to see AC/DC on their *Back in Black* tour. I didn't see them as part of the boring old-fart brigade. They were incredible. I'd never had music physically pummel me like theirs did. It was very, very, very loud but it didn't kill my ears, it hit me squarely in the body. Absolutely exhilarating.

The Ramones at Festival Hall was an eye-opener. Thousands of people in full punk regalia packed the room. This was Brisbane in 1980. Where the fuck did they all come from?! I'd never before or since seen so many leather jackets in one place.

The Ramones kicked my face in! 1–2–3–4! Bang! 1–2–3–4! Bang!

On it went.

My mind was made up. I would cut my hair and ask Mum to take ALL my jeans in. No more flares, no more Hawaiian shirts, no more old-fart bands.

Shortly after this gig I spent the afternoon at my friend Ben's place piercing my ear. Using an ice cube as a way to dull my earlobe, he put a wine cork behind it and poked a safety pin through. He was no expert and it took what seemed like hours. It was painful and messy. Blood everywhere.

When my mother saw it she flipped and kicked me out. Twenty-four hours later she begged me to come back. Well, in truth, she insisted I come home. A compromise was met when I opted for a *real* ear ring instead of a safety pin.

I had a girlfriend at the time. But two weeks after my punk transformation, it was over.

That hurt, but there was no going back now.

THE IDIOT

I first heard Iggy Pop's *The Idiot* when my brother played it on our family stereo.

I'm pretty sure I didn't like it. But it intrigued me. I'd never heard anything remotely like it before. I looked at the cover, a black-and-white photo of a weird-looking guy on a beach at night. It was all grey and blurry and so was the music. I could feel a simultaneous attraction and repulsion. What was happening to me?

I'd felt this way once before. One night the family was watching *Countdown* while preparing for Sunday night dinner. Molly announced 'and now a new group, big in England, it's racing up the charts over there. My mates, The Sex Pistols with "Anarchy in the UK"'.

'I AM AN ANTICHRRRIST.'

'Good lord, turn that rubbish off!' said my mother and my father. Click. I stood for a moment staring at the blank screen. I had to see more. There was a tiny portable television in the end room. I casually sauntered down there and closed the door behind me. I quickly turned on the portable and its tiny black-and-white screen came to life. Flicking the channels to the ABC I managed to catch the last minute of this much reviled act. A battle raged inside my 12-year-old soul. REPULSION AND ATTRACTION AT THE VERY SAME MOMENT. Yuck . . . but yes!

The Idiot gave me that same feeling. Robert played this record quite a lot at first but then not so much. I hadn't heard it for a few years when I played it again for myself in 1980. Dense with mystery and atmosphere, *The Idiot* throbs and grinds with electronic drones, rock drums and sludgy wah wah guitar. Iggy mostly sings in a strange monotone baritone but occasionally lets rip with an anguished scream.

I didn't own this copy of *The Idiot, The Idiot* owned ME. It had a deep and lasting effect and taught me many things, even how to sing. The song 'Dum Dum Boys' was why I called The Dum Dums, The Dum Dums.

Oh, and just because in May of that year, this record had been on the turntable of Joy Division's Ian Curtis when he was found hanged, doesn't mean it's depressing, but do be careful.

A PLACE CALLED
BAD

Queensland in the early '80s was a pretty silly place.

People go on about Premier Joh Bjelke-Petersen and the police state but if you ask me Bjelke-Petersen was a product of Queensland. Not the other way around. Queensland got what it deserved. Most people loved him. The people who didn't like the way he ran the state made a noise but they were a small minority. From what I could sense the majority of people accepted the situation and liked things the way they were. And it wasn't just the government and police. For me and plenty of others the general population was out to get you too.

There was a definite conservative, and dare I say it, apartheid feel about Brisbane in those days. It felt old and straight and regimented. Barren of colour or culture, and for most people, that was just lovely. For the ones that didn't think it was okay – usually gays, students and Aboriginal people – it was intolerable and repressive. Not many people got publicly angry about it but the ones who did got VERY angry. There was an attitude of resistance. It was the perfect atmosphere for breeding anti-establishment revolutionaries. I mean, lefties love a struggle, and here we had the most right-wing regressive government in Australia, so really, it was perfect. Each side justified the other's existence – the authorities could say, 'Look at those scumbags!' and the protesters could say, 'Look at those fascists'. Everyone's happy.

In those days kids like me would always get abused walking down the street and were regularly beaten up. That was just a fact of life. If I was alone on a train late at night and a bunch of guys got on I knew I was gonna cop a beating. They were going to lay into me until we got to the next stop.

Then start again when the train kept-a-rollin'.

It wasn't a skinhead thing or anything like that. It was just late 1970s, early 1980s Brisbane yobs. Guys in singlets and flared jeans and thongs. There was no tribal subculture thing to it. These guys were just cunts. And it was something you had to be aware of all the time. *Cunts were everywhere.*

And this was way before I chose to express myself with an *alternative look*. I got beat up before I was a punk and when I was a punk. Being beaten up for being a punk was better, at least there was a reason. All you had to do was have short hair and wear gym boots and you were singled out. People in cars would yell and scream serious abuse. You didn't have to be strutting around with a pink mohawk to get people going. All you had to be was just the tiniest bit different and you were in for it.

I never learned how to fight, but I learned how to get beat up. There was always more of them than me. That's how they hunted. Against three or four of these droogs you just did your best. I normally just had to cop it and try to lessen the likelihood of losing teeth by protecting my face with my arms.

This is a mentality I've never come close to understanding. Sure I've been in fights and when provoked I've wanted to do serious damage to the provocateur. But cold-bloodily seeking other humans to do harm to is beyond even my dark, angry heart. Yet, I saw a lot of it back then.

One night I got off the train and foolishly walked past a bunch of guys instead of heading in the opposite direction. Before I knew it I was smacked in the face. Still reeling from the hit, I took off. They pursued me. It was like sport for them. They chased me up the railway tracks, over back fences, across yards, and down deserted suburban streets. Finally, I spotted a taxi and ran for it. But the driver saw me coming and by the time I got to the car he'd wound up his windows, locked the door and drove off.

I kept running, the yob pack howling behind me.

This kind of violence was in the suburbs and the outskirts of the city. *Punk bashing* became a very popular blood sport of the time. Groups of dudes would deliberately go out and find a punk to bash.

If a bunch of punk rockers had a party there was no way it would end well. Inevitably a bunch of cars would pull up and a whole lot of guys would pile out, storm in and start smashing things up. Then they'd drag people out of the party and start laying into them. Just to teach us *a lesson.* I have no idea what the lesson was meant to be – but it was probably don't look like a punk or a poof.

To look like a punk rocker was pretty easy. Short hair, jeans that weren't flares and a t-shirt with a band name on it. I'd write the name of some band on the shirt myself in felt pen or scrawl Iggy and The Stooges on a jacket in house paint.

It's funny but I actually have some nostalgia for those times. There was a lot of horrible, awful, nasty, ugly, boring stuff . . . but I wouldn't call it tragic.

One night I was arrested in the city.

I was outside a place called White Chairs, a bar where anybody a bit weird or alternative would go. It closed at 10 pm so everyone would gather outside when the bar shut. We'd stand around on the footpath considering our next move. Nothing more provocative than that. This night there was maybe 20 people milling around trying to decide what to do next. And I think, without even raising my voice, I said something like, 'ah fuck it, let's just go.'

The next thing I knew a guy in a Hawaiian shirt, obviously a plain-clothes cop, grabbed me and arrested me for – *using obscene language in a public place.* I was led to a police car and taken to the watch house. I was wearing my Iggy and The Stooges jacket at the time.

One of the cops leers at me, 'The Stooges? Which one are you, dickhead – Larry, Curly or Moe?'

'Shemp,' I replied.

As we arrived at the police station, there was a bunch of cops hanging at the front desk. One of them looked at me and said, 'Fuck he's skinny isn'ee? And he looks like he's got drugs – strip-search him.' So they strip-searched me and I stood completely naked right there in the foyer of the police station in front of everybody and anybody. Then I was photographed and finger-printed and told I'd be held in a cell until somebody turned up with fifty bucks to pay my bail. All this for saying the word 'fuck' in a conversation with friends.

Why were they doing it? What was their purpose? Was it really revenue raising to get fifty dollars out of me? At the time none of these questions occurred to me. This sort of senseless-ness seemed so regular it was almost mundane.

Did I have the choice to go to court and defend the charges? Maybe I did, but I certainly wasn't told that by these filth. Who would bother anyway?

Thank fuck for my friend Michael Gilmore and his girl-friend who turned up a few hours later and paid my bail. Fifty bucks was a lot of money in 1981.

Michael knew the drill, he used to get arrested himself every couple of weeks. I saw him get nabbed walking back from The Clash concert at Cloudland. There was a mango tree hanging over the footpath and a mango had fallen into the street. Michael picked it up and tossed it a few feet in front of us and within seconds a siren went off and the boys in blue were there. Michael was bundled into a cop car and disappeared.

Stuff like this wasn't devastating. It was just weird and stupid, and I'd already seen weird, stupid, horrible, mundane, injustice at school and woken up to the fact that this was a continuation in the real word. This was just Brisbane.

MUSIC IS SPORT

I'd found out fast that signwriting has absolutely nothing to do with English . . . or Art.

It was about meticulous lines and squared-off edges . . . and cleanliness! And sure enough, rather than lead me into an apprenticeship it led me into working at screen-printing places as the Broom Boy, sweeping floors and getting lunches.

Over the next 12 months I had a half-dozen different jobs. Most of them would last exactly eight weeks. For the first four weeks, I would be a model employee, turning up on time and doing a decent job. After that I'd get comfortable and started turning up a little late, five minutes at first, then 15, until I thought I deserved a day off. By the seventh week my employers realised who they were dealing with and I was out the door at the end of the eighth.

For a time, I worked at a furniture warehouse where I started as storeman, delivery boy and showroom salesman. A 15-year-old kid – me! – as a showroom salesman. No training. No info. No idea. Idiots!

I was supposed to greet customers, sometimes whole families, as they came in. Then I'd answer their questions about furniture. But I had no idea what I was talking about. A guy would come in and ask me about a mattress. *What is it made of? Is it waterproof? Do you have a repayment plan?*

I'd look at them and say, 'You know what? If I was you I'd be sleeping on this foam one – it's twenty bucks.' Their next question was inevitable.

'Is there anyone else I can speak to?'

I was feeling set adrift, with no connection to anything. So when my mate Gary said, 'Let's go sign up at the local football club,' I thought, 'Why not? I'm not doing much else.' The local club was the Sandgate Hawks Australian Football Club. The attraction for Gary and I wasn't really the football. We had heard a rumour that they let you drink.

Until then I hadn't even watched a game of Aussie Rules on TV but I threw myself into the deep end. They were a good bunch of blokes and through gritted teeth they endured me, and I in turn endured their impatience with me trying to get the hang of the game. Usually, I started on the bench and they put me on the field for ten minutes here and there then got me off quick.

I really had no idea what I was doing. At no stage had I actually said to anyone that I didn't know ANY of the rules

SANDGATE AUSTRALIAN FOOTBALL CLUB
UNDER SEVENTEEN GRADE
SEMI-FINALISTS 1980

of this game. On the other hand, no one sat down with me and offered to explain what you can and can't do. This was the under 17s. I was the only beginner. But they didn't tell me even the most basic rules – the stuff about needing to handball, or oh shit, you've got to bounce the thing when you run?

I bluffed my way through the entire season, with limited success.

Yes, I did a whole season of footy while slowly gaining only the slightest idea of what the hell was going on. But let's not kid ourselves – this was not about football. It was really about a bunch of teenagers drinking a keg in the dressing room on Saturday night after the game and getting really, really throwing-up drunk.

Straight after the season was over I got into rock'n'roll and didn't look back.

Footy season was over and music took my complete focus. Sport and rock were never comfortable bedfellows, and for the next 13 years, I denied having any knowledge of any sport of any kind. No one I knew from that point even mentioned it.

Around this age I started to go out to gigs and see bands. I'd tell my parents, 'Might go to bed a little early tonight,' followed by a very convincing yawn. Then I would carefully remove the louvred windows in my bedroom, climb through and quietly steal away through the backyards of suburban Boondall, down to the train station and off into town.

There wasn't a real lot going on in Brisbane around this time. Or certainly it didn't seem like there was to me. Brisbane had given birth to the 'world's first punk rock band' The Saints a few years prior, for which we should all be grateful, but by the time I was out there The Saints had left for England and were considered traitors for deserting us. There was a FUCK THE SAINTS attitude. Brisbane hated people that left. The Leftovers were the punk band that never left Brisbane. They were in the Sex Pistols mould of punk bands. Safety pins, leather jackets, crime, drugs, suicide and all the trimmings. True scum. But all that was long over by the time I was venturing into the Brisbane night in 1981.

Decent gigs were scarce, so when there was one, you just had to go. Maybe if I'd been part of some scene I'd have known about more, but I wasn't. There were only one or two places I knew about around Fortitude Valley and the city centre – the

White Chairs bar and The Exchange Hotel where I saw The Go-Betweens and Laughing Clowns without knowing who they were at the time. It didn't really matter what band was on where, I'd just go.

Of course I was under-age, but I had no problem getting in. I was tall.

It wasn't always a trip into town either. Occasionally I went deeper into the suburbs. The Homestead Hotel was a large beer barn in Zillmere, a suburb not far from Boondall. One night in 1980 I went to see The Radiators. Flannelette and corduroy were everywhere. The place was packed with suburban kids drunk and going wild. Forget the punks and new wavers, this lot really knew how to fuck shit up!

The room for rock concerts was also used for wedding receptions so the venue had rows of long trestle tables set up around the perimeter. The dance floor was packed so the rest of us got up on these tables for a better vantage point. No one asked us to get down, so more and more punters got up. As the show intensified, we jumped harder and higher, until the inevitable happened and the tables collapsed. It was exhilarating. A dozen kids fell in a heap on the floor, the band played on, no one even noticed. No one got hurt; we all roared with laughter, then launched ourselves back into the fray, mullets and desert boots flying everywhere. It was like a giant rumpus room for drunk teenagers. Magnificent!

As I started getting away from home more, I started meeting people. There was this girl I used to see on the train. I think her name was Michelle. She would be waiting for the same train, often heading in to the same gig. She was the only one on the train that had new wave clothes on, so we made a connection.

We were never boyfriend and girlfriend or anything like that, but we used to go to gigs together. At one of these gigs we met up with these two guys, Glen and Shane. Out of the blue they asked if we wanted to be in their band. They said they already had a gig lined up. It was going to be at the Queensland Uni in the city. The name of their band? The Corpse of Christ.

We did a rudimentary rehearsal where there were a few riffs and ideas thrown around, but we never actually fired up all together. Instead we just sat around discussing music we liked. The general idea of the band was . . . well, I can't remember if there was a general idea. Glen and Shane were into bands I didn't know very much about at the time – Throbbing Gristle and other industrial, avant-garde things. But we shared a love for The Stooges.

So just for being wide-eyed and up for anything, Michelle and I found ourselves joining The Corpse of Christ. And yes, there was a gig. A real gig, for THIS band. A band that included ME.

On the night of the show we were all insanely nervous and when we finally got onstage, everything we had spoken about went out the window and it became this completely ridiculous shamble. Just noise. In fact not even connected enough to be deliberate noise.

Nobody realised until the 'music' began that Michelle couldn't drum to save her life. She sat behind the kit limply flapping the sticks across the skins and cymbals. I was on guitar and, realising it had all gone to hell, started goosestepping across the stage while bashing away on my $50 guitar, oblivious to the other members of the band and in, I'm not sure what state of mind.

It was awful on a scale many people had never witnessed before. Let's not try to gloss this over. It was dreadful.

After a while my good friend Michael Gilmore, who was sitting close to the stage, beckoned me over. 'You should stop now!' he shouted in my ear. We didn't. People politely booed until it was over.

At the end of the gig we went our separate ways. With all of us quite aware of just how unimpressed the world had been with our debut, Glen called a 'band meeting' a few days later. With a few beers in their bellies, he and Shane told us they were going to change the name of the band and were considering maybe going on as a duo. There's no way to put this any differently, but Michelle and I were 'let go' from The Corpse of Christ.

I knew it was coming, and fank thuck it did.

DUM DUM

Not long after my stint — can you call one gig a stint? — with The Corpse of Christ I started hanging out with people who took . . . drugs.

I didn't know much about drugs. It was a very experimental stage, and I was being given things I really had no idea about, or what they were going to do to me. But I was open-eyed and trusting so I smoked, slurped and swallowed what I was handed.

One night a few of us were going out and somebody had a Serepax. I didn't really know what a Serepax was. I know now it's a sleeping pill.

I think it was a pretty low dosage I took this night but I was drunk and I fairly rapidly became this completely obnoxious buffoon as the pill came on. In fact I can say that this night

I was THE MOST OBNOXIOUS PIECE OF SHIT ON THE PLANET. It was a gig at the Communist Hall and a band called Pork were playing. I was sort of watching them but mostly yelling at them, and knocking things over everywhere as I stumbled around. I wasn't being violent but I was completely unaware of my surroundings and I was casually creating havoc.

Eventually I fell down this incredibly long staircase and just lay there awhile as no one would dare come near me, let alone check on my wellbeing. I wasn't really hurt and if I was, I sure wasn't feeling it. I actually tried to pick a fight with someone while I was laying on the ground at the foot of these stairs so I copped a bit of a kicking into the bargain.

Oh, what fun.

A few weeks later I was at another club and two guys came over.

'Are you the guy from the Pork gig at the Communist Hall the other night?' one asked me. I sheepishly admitted that, *Yes it was me.*

'Do you want to be in a band with us?'

Sure, why not?

I may be paraphrasing a little there, but that's how I remember it. The guys were Greg and Ian Wadley. Ian was 16 and Greg 18. These two sweet geeks *discovered* me, if 'discovered' is the right word. Certainly, if 'discovery' is watching a fucking idiot be obnoxious in a public place then they can rightly lay claim to it. Obviously they saw my potential, a potential I had no idea of. A potential for what? They figured, as a frontman. And as a result we formed The Dum Dums.

'I'm not like that ALL the time,' I warned them.

'We'll see,' says Greg. (Yes, but which Greg?)

In The Dum Dums there were four of us – Ian Wadley, Greg Wadley, Greg Perkins and Greg Gilbert. That's three Gregs in the band which is ridiculous. We nearly called ourselves Ian and The Gregs. Clearly though there were too many Gregs. Nothing was really said but before we even played a note of music together we all knew we could easily lose one, in name at least.

By now it's 1981 and there's a whole thing going on of making up identities and adopting punk rock names: Johnny Rotten, Sid Vicious, Lux Interior, Rat Scabies and so on, and on a local level, Ed Wreckage, Johnny Burnaway and V2.

Making up punk-rock noms de plume was an occasional pastime. We came up with things like Mars Blowfly and Grit Savage.

Yes, readers, I could easily have become known as Grit Savage. Trust me, it was close.

We started a graffiti campaign based around the name Grit Savage. We'd paint Grit Savage on the sides of buildings and on toilet walls. Slogans like *Grit Savage has gone*, *Grit Savage is a great guy*, *Grit Savage has his own teeth*. But my favourite was *Pumpkins, Carrots, Potatoes, Cabbage – Everybody Loves . . . Grit Savage*.

Amid this culture of making up silly names, 'Tex Deadly' came up.

It was Greg Wadley who pushed the hand of fate. I remember him saying, 'Hmmm, that one's not bad.' Greg was a bit older than the rest of us and was also in another band called The Pits who were doing pretty good business in the Brisbane underground at the time. So he was the one with all the connections and was booking all our gigs. Greg saw himself as a bit of a Malcolm McLaren-type figure and liked to 'make things happen' so the next time Greg booked us a gig it was as Tex Deadly and The Dum Dums.

Overnight that became our new name. There was no band meeting. I wasn't even consulted. One day I saw one of our gig posters. There it was: Tex Deadly and The Dum Dums.

Of course it very quickly became assumed and apparent that as frontman I would be known as Tex Deadly. And to be honest that seemed like fun to me. After all, I wore kinda punk rock cowboy clothes, and I was tall and bow-legged and I listened to Johnny Cash. So the name Tex fit, and it stuck.

Like many other things, I didn't put a moment's thought into what that would mean in the long term. I should've known that for the rest of my days I would be asked the question, 'Is that your real name?', or 'Are you from Texas?' I didn't consider it then, but this nom de plume would ensure that I was never quite taken seriously, and a great many assumptions would be made of me because of it. Oh well.

What was the music of Tex Deadly and The Dum Dums like, you ask? Well people always mention words like *cowpunk* and *psychobilly*. We were that, I guess, but mainly we were very, very NOISY. *Trashy* is a better word for our sound. *Sloppybilly* – might even be better yet. How about *Sillybilly?* Yeah, that's it.

We had original songs like 'Cough it Up', 'This Here Country' and 'Cheap Funerals', but we also did a lot of covers. The first gig's set list included Johnny Cash's 'Ring of Fire' and 'Dirt' by The Stooges. And because The Cramps were THE band for me at the time we did covers that The Cramps covered like 'The Way I Walk' and 'Green Door', songs by Johnny Burnette and Screamin' Jay Hawkins, and music inspired by the trash culture of Russ Meyer and John Waters films. For Tex Deadly and The Dum Dums anything with a simple structure to it was good, and from there we found a rockabilly groove as our knowledge grew.

Let's face it; we were pretty terrible, but at the time it was hard to tell. Now, when I listen back to recordings of early Dum Dums shows it's all harsh tinny feedback, also the tunings were dodgy at best. And that's just the singing.

But it was my first *real* band. It was shambolic – and glorious.

The most important thing was the primitive simplicity of it – and the trashy humour. Put those things together and it was perfect . . . in its own way.

I hadn't bothered writing anything of note since school, but when you're in a band you need songs, so you don't so much 'write' them as explain them to your band mates and then you see where it goes. That's what I did anyway.

One of the early Dum Dums song was a thing called 'Cough It Up'. I probably 'wrote it' with this explanation.

'Okay, I need an intro . . . maybe just stay on one note for a while . . . maybe some cymbals sizzling . . . then I'll do a spoken word intro about a heavy smoker getting some bad news at the doctors . . . okay, and when I say, "DOC WHAT CAN I DO?" and he says "Nothin'!" you guys break into a 12-bar . . . really thrash it out! . . . and I'll cough all the way through . . . okay?'

And that's pretty much what we did.

The first *good* song I was involved with was a tune Ian Wadley brought to me. I wrote the lyrics and it became 'This Here Country', a kind of a cowboy song parody. A great band from Melbourne, The Sacred Cowboys, had done a similar thing with 'Nothin' Grows in Texas'. Ours was much sillier.

One of the next 'songs' I 'wrote' was a thing called 'Ten Wheels For Jesus'. Musically I arrived at the song's riff one day as I was fooling around on a guitar trying to play Alan Vega's song 'Magdalena'. Unable to play that song my inept fingers led me in an unintentional direction, where I suddenly thought, 'That's not "Magdalena", but that's not bad.' Lyrically, the idea was to sound like the religious rants of an evangelical disease-ridden truck driver. When a truck driver has only ten wheels it means he is carrying no load. He is free, he's unhindered and unhinged. The other influence on that song was the Legendary Stardust Cowboy, but we were too good to really play like that.

During those years I was just looking around at everything that was going on. The first time I'd seen The Scientists was a bit like the first time I heard The Cramps. It was *OF COURSE. THAT'S HOW IT'S DONE.* I had heard the 'Swampland/ Happy Hour' single and liked it but when I saw the band live it ticked *all* the boxes. They looked and sounded like the perfect rock band. Wild hairdos, weird clothes and a gang mentality. The Scientists had The Stooges' heavy riffing, the swamp sound of The Cramps and Creedence Clearwater Revival, plus Kim playing slide guitar and harmonica and Tony doing the fuzz guitar. I worshipped them. The first time I saw The Birthday Party was the same, and they were incredibly exciting.

The Birthday Party were impressive and I knew it was unique and everything, but with The Scientists the penny dropped harder for me.

Our first gig as Tex Deadly and The Dum Dums was at the New York Hotel in Brisbane. It was this ornate carpeted place, not particularly rock'n'roll. The New York could hold maybe five or six hundred people, but the most significant thing was the height of the stage. It was maybe 12 feet above the dance floor and around the sides was a mezzanine/balcony section so there were a lot of good vantage points.

This was the first of those sweet gigs that Greg Wadley's connections won us. We were on the bill with a Sydney ska band called The Allniters who were kind of a big deal at that time and were managed by a fast-talking, in-your-face guy called Roger Grierson. The Dum Dums went on first.

I was nervous, much more nervous than the last time I'd been on a stage (which was the first time, with Corpse of Christ). Now I was the frontman, I clutched that microphone stand like it was part of my life support system!

I managed to make it to the end of the set without throwing up or passing out. The Wadleys were disappointed I didn't display any of the reckless antics they'd seen at the Pork gig. But that would come soon enough.

After we played, this Roger fellow came up to me and said he liked the show and that we should come to Sydney and play some gigs. He just gave us his phone number and urged us to get in touch.

Let's pause. This is a pivotal moment in our story, dear reader.

If Roger hadn't seen us that night nothing may have ever happened. Well, *something* might've happened but maybe *everything that DID happen*, wouldn't have. To be

DDP PRESENTS

DANCE
WITH
THE END
☆
PLAYERS PLEASE TWIST
☆
TEX DEADLY & THE DUM-DUMS
☆
MISSING WORDS
☆
FRI 19TH NOV

SOUTH'S LEAGUES CLUB HALL
RIVER END, JANE St, WEST END
DOORS OPEN 7:30 PM - $5 zzz $4

honest I'm astounded Roger felt that way about us because I'm pretty sure we were terrible, but like Greg Wadley maybe he saw POTENTIAL.

Brisbane was a real slog for a band like us, despite Greg's connections. Apart from a gig at the New York or one of the other larger venues, or swinging a support spot with a touring band, there weren't many places to play or opportunities to grow. You could put on your own gigs, hire a hall, put a PA in and do everything yourself. We'd done that a bit already but in Sydney there was what seemed like hundreds of gigs. So we rang Roger and hey, he wasn't lying. The gigs were *waiting for us*. We got hold of a Dodge van with no back seats and piled everything into it. We taped DUM DUMS down the side in masking tape and got on the highway. I was 17. The big town down south beckoned. In the end it was like the Ramones had told us: LEAVE HOME.

MY CITY OF SYDNEY

Sydney in the early '80s was just wonderful.

Coming from early '80s Brisbane, this place seemed like New York! It was a real city with cool people – and by 'cool people' I mean people that weren't complete arseholes. In Brisbane I was still this awkward kid dragging my childhood and past around with me. But moving to Sydney I had a clean slate and everyone responded to me differently. It really felt like I was starting my life over again. I was no longer in a place where everyone was spitting or sneering at me or putting me down in some way.

I'm not saying that what happened in Brisbane wasn't important. All that struggle helped make me what I am (a deeply scarred sociopath with anger management issues).

But in Sydney I found an acceptance and a respect I had never known before. Everyone I met in Sydney at that time – I love all those people to this day. Those people embraced me. I was this punk kid, new to town, but there was none of that 'You're that dickhead kid' I'd always get in Brisbane. In Sydney I was a 17-year-old singer with a fresh start in a rock'n'roll band.

Sydney circa 1982 was humming. There were so many venues in the outer suburbs as well as a really healthy inner city underground scene. People look at me like I'm from another planet when I say that a band could play five or six nights a week in Sydney. There were suburban venues and scenes every-where – and so many other places all over the city.

And around the centre of Sydney was just magnificent. The epicentres of the alternative, underground scene were the Southern Cross Hotel down near Central railway station in Surry Hills, and the Sydney Trade Union Club a couple of blocks over.

The Southern Cross – which later became the Strawberry Hills Hotel – was run by this cool old guy (well, he seemed old to me) called Ron Audas and he had help from his son Gary. It was a small place but pretty much every local and interstate band I wanted to see played there. Music was performed seven nights a week and it was free to get in . . . I think.

The Sydney Trade Union Club – the Trades – on Foveaux Street was indie-rock central. I ended up playing there many, many times. EVERYONE went to the Trades. You joined up, got a badge and went crazy. The place was open till 7 am. Bands were on the top floor which held several hundred people. Then on the middle floor had cabaret and pool tables and stuff, and the ground floor was for the pokies and serious all-night drinking. This was where you ended up after floors two and three had closed down for the night.

Tex Deadly and The Dum Dums played all over Sydney. In the early days we were unprepared for the effect we had on people. We *were* a little irreverent and I don't know if a lot of people knew how to take us. The truth was we weren't asking to be taken seriously. Spectacle and humour were more important to us than good songs and great playing. So in those first months in Sydney the few people who came and saw us thought, 'What the fuck are they on about?'

That was summed up by one gig I will always remember at this place in the middle of the city just off Pitt Street. There's a shopping arcade that runs through to George Street called the Strand Arcade and downstairs was a really popular night-club at the time called Stranded. We were the support slot for The Scientists.

So I'm leaving the stage after our set and making my way to the band room when this fellow steps in front of me and screams:

'I HATE YOU!

'I HATE YOUR BAND!!

'YOU MADE A MOCKERY OF ALL MY FAVOURITE MUSIC.

'FUCK YOU!!!'

And then he stormed off.

When I get back to the band room everyone looks up at me and asks, 'What did Dave Faulkner say to you?'

'Who's Dave Faulkner?'

'The guy from the Hoodoo Gurus. They're the biggest band around.'

'Oh, him? HE LOVES US!'

Dave's was probably the most hysterical reaction we got, but it was not altogether uncommon.

Were Tex Deadly and The Dum Dums for real? Was this a joke band? No one could get their head around the fact that I seemed to be right into what I was doing . . . but taking the piss at the same time.

Affectionate disrespect was a difficult concept in the post punk scene.

The first time I met Kim Salmon, then fronting The Scientists, he approached me, not aggressively or condescendingly, but genuinely curious as to whether we were serious or not.

I couldn't tell him. I'd never thought about it.

Over the next 12 months or so The Dum Dums changed personnel a few times over. The final line-up had no Wadleys and not even any Gregs.

Marco, Ceril and Fruitcake were a 'crack unit', a far cry from the wobbly twang of the early Brisbane line-up – this was fast, tight rockabilly. These guys could actually play. Thankfully we could also still piss people off.

Sometimes we'd play a support set for one of the bigger bands on the scene like The Johnnys, The Cockroaches, The Allniters when they ventured out into the suburbs. At these band barns the beer cans were thrown so often when

Tex Deadly and The Dum Dums were on, we grew to hardly notice them. One night I said to the crowd, 'Hey look, throwing cans is one thing, but if you really hate us throw money! A fifty-cent piece could really hurt!'

'Ha ha,' went the band. 'Good one Tex.'

Next thing, coins of all denominations are being hurled at the stage with vicious intent! We played two more songs in a hail of shrapnel and then split. The rest of the band were not happy, but we made an extra $47 that night.

The Dum Dums continued on for a while and then at some stage Marco got the shits and without a word just left town. I think his decision was partly based on me not doing my share of the lugging-equipment-side of things, but I think it was more the old story of the guitar player getting jealous of the attention the singer's getting that they feel should be directed towards them.

Sorry Marco.

Bye bye Marco.

The Dum Dums stopped dead after that. However, there were a few gigs booked so when Tex Deadly and The Dum Dums fell apart I hatched a plan to honour those commitments and get the money I could sorely use.

Now all I needed was a band . . .

BEASTS OF BOURBON

Since coming to Sydney I'd found myself gravitating to older dudes — musicians that'd been around the block once or twice.

These elder statesmen of the scene became like big brothers to me . . . and I mean the best kind of big brother, not the kind that hold you down and fart in your face.

Spencer P. Jones and Boris Sudjovic were two such characters. These guys looked out for me and I looked up to them. So when I mentioned the vacant Dum Dums gigs, Spencer and Boris were only too happy to get on board.

The P in Spencer P. Jones stands for Patrick. When I first met him he had just arrived in Sydney to join The Johnnys, a rock'n'roll band that dressed as cowboys. The Johnnys didn't play country or western; they played New York Dolls-style rock'n'roll that had cowboy song titles. They'd been a three piece, but Jonesy was called in to broaden their horizons, musically and otherwise. In retrospect it was more a handing over of the keys. Rod Radalj would leave The Johnnys soon after Spencer arrived. Rod has been a founding member of The Scientists, the Hoodoo Gurus, The Johnnys and the Dubrovniks but every time, just when the band starts to get somewhere, Rod splits.

Back then Spencer was hungry for everything and one of the funniest, most mischievous scallywags around. We became friends right away. He was a Kiwi, although you'd never know it. By the time I met him he'd been on the Yob Continent for over a decade and there was no trace of THAT accent. Look, I love New Zealand – it's a great little country we Aussies could learn a lot from . . . but *that accent*. Fuck me. But I digress.

Spencer Jones was, and always will be, family to me. You know how you can treat your family badly and still expect them to be there? That's Spencer. In the 35 years that followed our initial meeting we would endure some truly shitty times when we didn't think much of each other but I will never not, at the heart of it, love Spencer. After the dung has been flung between us, we're still family.

Spencer and I shared a flat on Crown Street in Darlinghurst for a time. We were harmonious flatmates, as we rarely saw each other. The Johnnys worked *a lot*. In fact that year we first met they did more shows than there were days in the year.

One day I was trying to clean up the kitchen. Our frying pan was thick with fat, so I thought I'd heat it up a bit to make the fat easier to remove. I went to the lounge room to grab some plates and when I returned there were flames three feet high roaring from the pan. Without thinking I threw the frying pan out the window, scaring the shit out of the Vietnamese family in the flat below. Spencer had come into the room just as the pan left my hand and, as the family's screams took flight, he shot me a look and deadpanned, 'Tex, that's the only uncool thing I've ever seen you do.'

I'm sorry to say there would be many more.

Boris Sudjovic was the affable one in The Scientists. Brett Rixon hid behind a curtain of hair and would only speak when absolutely necessary. Tony Thewlis had a fuzz box and Johnny Thunders' hairdo so he didn't need to say anything either.

But Boris I got to know and like. He was a big guy with big hair and he wore shirts louder than the bands he was in.

Boris was another brother I feel grateful to for being a good friend back then. We would run into each other at the Southern Cross Hotel or the Trade Union Club at all hours of the day. He had my back and I had his. That made him a perfect band mate.

These gigs needed doing and all of us, as usual, needed money. No big deal.

But the venue needed a name for the band.

Now a few weeks before there'd been an article I'd seen in a magazine about The Gun Club – a band we all really liked. The photo of the band that went with the story had them sharing a bottle of whiskey and the headline was 'Beasts Of Bourbon'. I looked at it and said 'there's a band name'. Now I'd been put on the spot for a band name, that one seemed pretty good . . . for now.

So we put together this band and called it The Beasts Of Bourbon.

A lot of people think that the name came about because we were bourbon drinkers – but we weren't. When it came to alcohol the Beasts were fuelled by beer. Believe it or not, people used to drink Foster's back then.

People also think it was our play on 'Beast Of Burden' by the Rolling Stones but that's bullshit. At that stage I hadn't even heard that song.

Honestly, at the time we thought it was a throwaway band name for a bunch of guys who'd gotten together to play a couple of shows and we'd have it for maybe two or three nights then we'd move on with the rest of our lives.

So it was that Spencer, Boris and I, along with Fruitcake, played the Southern Cross Hotel in Surry Hills one night in June 1983 as The Beasts Of Bourbon. Along with a few tunes from the Dum Dums set, we fleshed out the rest of the show with covers of Cramps, Gun Club, Stones and Stooges songs. That first gig was easy and fun. It had a heaviness that had always eluded the Dum Dums. *People loved it.*

After that gig more offers rolled in, and it was very easy to say yes.

The Beasts line-up changed at each of the remaining gig commitments. Fruitcake was replaced by, believe it or not, Richard Ploog of The Church and then he was replaced by James Baker.

James was actually 11 years older than me so less a big brother and more a kind of father figure. A cheery, bleary, boozy father figure.

He and his partner Susan would often give me a decent meal when I was broke. They were among the few people I knew that had a nice clean house and they often shared it with me. I loved them both and without their generosity things would've been much harder for me in those early years in Sydney.

James had been a rocker since the early '70s, and in his travels

Me on stage with the Beasts, 1984.

had managed to be in New York at the time the Ramones and Television were taking off. Then he'd landed in London when the Sex Pistols, The Clash and the Damned were starting. When I met him he must have been in his late twenties but he was (and still is) an eternal teenager, a true rock'n'roller and one of the coolest, most easygoing guys I've ever known.

When Kim Salmon joined, the classic Beasts line-up was complete.

Kim had approached me a few years earlier at a Dum Dums gig by saying, 'Hey, look I don't want this to sound offensive, but ... *are you serious?*' These were the first words he ever said to me. I didn't have an answer and I don't think I even understood the question. All I knew was I was talking to the lead singer of my favourite band.

The Scientists were a different kettle of fish than the gregarious Johnnys. They were virtual rock snobs by comparison. They exuded a quiet arrogance, as if they knew they were the best band in the country. That was fair enough, because they WERE the best band in the country. When they eventually *left* Australia to live in London, I took care of Congo, the Salmon family's pet poodle, until a few months later when I too went to live in that paradise they called Mother England.

Then, as now, Kim has often been baffled with my 'methods' but he must have seen something in me back then as we became good friends. I would learn that Kim was 'serious' about his fun.

For years later, people would always remind us that The Beasts Of Bourbon weren't really a proper band. We were a thrown-together posse of guys with a mercenary philosophy about us.

And sure, at first we were just banging it together to make a couple of bucks. Nobody thought we were going to be doing this for very long. It was just the way it was – the Beasts united if somebody had a good enough offer and we'd fill the band with whoever was available at the time.

But after we'd fulfilled those handful of Dum Dums gigs we started to get a bit of momentum. Everyone was still doing their own gigs in their own bands but the Beasts had buzz and the offers to play got better and better.

Right from the start The Beasts Of Bourbon had this undeniable appeal. Each of us was a distinctive character and all of us were good players in our own right. It was easy to publicise a band featuring members of the Hoodoo Gurus, The Scientists and The Johnnys. I'm not sure being a former member of Tex Deadly and The Dum Dums added much cache but the other guys did.

With the Beasts there was no real discussion about a unified image or anything like that. The band's image was pretty much established by *who* was in the band because everyone had established their own individual image via the other bands they'd been in.

Together as Beasts Of Bourbon we made this big, swaggering blues/swamp sound and became a certified indie underground supergroup.

And inadvertently we had created a great rock'n'roll band.

THE AXEMAN'S JAZZ

The Beasts Of Bourbon was a big deal to a bunch of people fairly quickly and didn't take long to catch fire as a thing.

Pretty soon after it took off, Roger Grierson, ever the entrepreneur, piped up to say we should capitalise on this thing we had because it might not last very long. Roger figured the Beasts were a zeitgeist band, a moment in time that should be recorded, so he booked a studio in Woolloomooloo for us to record an album and got producer Tony Cohen on board to record us.

Tony had recorded a lot of significant stuff in Melbourne in the mid-'70s through to the mid-'80s. He recorded things like The Ferrets' 'Don't Fall In Love', which became a big *Countdown* hit. He also did the classic 'I Like It Both Ways' by Supernaut. Basically Tony was a pop/rock guy who was a great engineer and had a good ear, which was why industry heavies like Molly Meldrum liked to work with him when they were producing.

Tony had worked his way up through a studio called Richmond Recorders. When the punk bands all appeared and started recording and using studios in Melbourne, Tony was usually the youngest guy in the studio scene so they all automatically gravitated to him because the sense was the young guy would be cool and into what those bands were trying to do.

And Tony *was* great with bands. He could relate to them and he was prepared to take chances and mess around with things in the studio. Most of the other studio dudes tended to be pretty rigid compared to him. Tony always brought a great vibe to his sessions. His enthusiasm was contagious. He wasn't one of those pricks that say, 'Hmmm, no I don't think we can do that.' Tony was the original 'Why not?' guy.

The original Beasts (from left to right): Kim Salmon, Spencer P. Jones, James Baker, Boris Sujdovic and me.

If you go back and listen to the stuff he worked on in the late '70s and early '80s you will hear some pretty amazing stuff. One of his best is The Birthday Party's album *Prayers On Fire* released in 1981. It's a really powerful mix – atmospheric, but tight and hard-hitting and dare I say, very funky. Things like 'Zoo Music Girl' groove along like nothin' else.

Tony's stories about the recording of *Prayers* and its follow-up *Junkyard* would curl your hair. Turns out Nick Cave and the gang were very fortunate to have school prefect Mick Harvey there to keep things focused and functioning. Tony was right in the middle of it too. He was always the right man in the right place at the right time . . . doing all the wrong things.

When Tony recorded The Birthday Party and Hunters & Collectors, The Sacred Cowboys and The Models' mini-album *Cut Lunch* he established a trademark bass sound. With Tony, the bass was the core instrument in any band. It wasn't merely a part of the rhythm section beefing up the background. The bass player was front and centre, riffing a hole in your gut. When we met Tony that day at Paradise studios, I knew none of this. I hadn't even thought about what a 'producer' was.

Up to this point the gigs the Beasts had been doing – and there hadn't been many of them – had required two, sometimes even three sets which means we needed to know lots of songs. Not surprisingly a lot of them were covers. Songs by people like Alice Cooper, Creedence Clearwater Revival, The Stooges and the New York Dolls.

Roger must have assumed we'd be doing a sort of covers record. A 'Sydney underground supergroup plays underground classics' kind of thing.

But something happened between the decision to record and actually doing it – we managed to find the time to write and the songs came quickly so by the time we got into the studio we had mostly original songs. I use the term *original* loosely. I'm not saying that album is full of rip-offs, but the way we'd 'write' a song back then would be to have a set of lyrics and then someone might say 'Let's try it like that Beefheart song "I'm Gonna Booglarize You Baby"' and off we'd go. 'Save me a place' indeed.

By tossing around ideas and referencing our vast collective knowledge of our favourite rock'n'roll records, an original song list came very naturally and fast. Everyone brought in one or two tunes. I had a couple left over from the Dum Dums – 'Ten Wheels For Jesus' and 'Lonesome Bones' – plus with 'Evil Ruby' I had a bunch of lyrics which Spencer suggested trying it as a Stones/Creedence stomp. It was a throw-it-against-the-wall attitude but thankfully enough managed to stick. Cos everyone knows that filth is sticky.

Spencer was hanging around at Roger Grierson and Stuart Coupe's house at the time – he may even have been living on the couch. Roger and Stuart lived in the downstairs floor of a two-storey place in Cathedral Street in Woolloomooloo. Upstairs were the offices of Regular Records – the hipper, more mainstream indie record label of the day. This place was Sydney rock central at the time if you were in bands like

From left to right: James Baker, Spencer P. Jones, Boris Sujdovic, me, Congo and Kim Salmon.

The Johnnys, The Allniters, the Hoodoo Gurus . . . or the nascent Beasts Of Bourbon. They all hung downstairs, while up above was the world of Icehouse, Mental As Anything . . . and Austen Tayshus.

Stuart had a massive collection of books and a lot of crime fiction. Spencer was leafing through one, *The Notebooks of Raymond Chandler*, and in it was one of the few poems that Chandler wrote – a piece called 'Song At Parting'. Spencer showed it to me. It was about a guy who killed a woman by leaving a meat axe in her brain. *Right up our alley.* So we figured there was a song in it . . .

Swamp was firmly where my own head was at. Swamps and graveyards were big with me at 17 or 18. I was very much embracing the whole idea of the American South, New Orleans music and all that voodoo culture. That's why Creedence Clearwater was such a big influence on me and why that first Beasts album became an extended ode to the Big Easy and all that Southern stuff. It's got murder, trains, trucks, drugs, swamps, graveyards, buses . . . and a few more murders.

Creedence is an important connection because they too had that obsession, but they weren't from the South. They were from San Francisco – hippie town – and yet they decided that their thing would be the South. That would be their schtick. They weren't from there but they wanted to fantasise about it because for them that was where it was at – the whole mythology of it. And I felt the same way.

Anyway, I'd seen a few swamps in my day.

The reason that the album is called *The Axeman's Jazz* is that someone I knew – I think it was Jules Normington – had a book called something like *Myths And Legends of New Orleans* and there was a chapter called 'The Axeman's Jazz'. It was about a serial killer in New Orleans just after World War I who was going around axing people. And his one passion in life apart from slicing and dicing people was jazz. So he wrote a letter to the local newspaper saying that he would not attack anyone in any house that was emitting jazz music. For a long time after that there was jazz coming from just about every house because everyone was in fear of the Axeman. This was the myth that we took the name from. The actual letter reads as follows:

Hell, May 6th, 1919

Esteemed Mortal:

They have never caught me and they never will. They have never seen me, for I am invisible, even as the ether that surrounds your earth. I am not a human being, but a spirit and a demon from the hottest hell. I am what you Orleanians and your foolish police call the Axeman.

When I see fit, I shall come and claim other victims. I alone know whom they shall be. I shall leave no clue except my bloody axe, besmeared with blood and brains of he whom I have sent below to keep me company.

. . . Undoubtedly, you Orleanians think of me as a most horrible murderer, which I am, but I could be much worse if I wanted to. If I wished, I could pay a visit to your city every night. At will I could slay thousands of your best citizens, for I am in close relationship with the Angel of Death.

Now, to be exact, at 12.15 (earthly time) on next Tuesday night, I am going to pass over New Orleans. In my infinite mercy, I am going to make a little proposition to you people. Here it is:

I am very fond of jazz music, and I swear by all the devils in the nether regions that every person shall be spared in whose home a jazz band is in full swing at the time I have mentioned. If everyone has a jazz band going, well, then, so much the better for you people. One thing is certain and that is that some of your people who do not jazz it on Tuesday night (if there be any) will get the axe.

Well, as I am cold and crave the warmth of my native Tartarus, and it is about time I leave your earthly home, I will cease my discourse . . . I have been, am and will be the worst spirit that ever existed either in fact or realm of fancy.

The Axeman

There's improvisation on *The Axeman's Jazz* but not a lot of jazz. It's a better title than *The Axeman's Blues* – we were closer to the blues, but *Axeman's Jazz* just sounds better, especially if you're not actually playing jazz. So no, there's not a whole lot of jazz but there is a whole lot of killin' on that record, some of it with axes, so it fit nicely. I think at least one person cops it in pretty much every song. From memory 'Drop Out' and 'Ten Wheels For Jesus' are the only songs where someone doesn't meet their end in some way (but with 15 kinds of diseases the protagonist in 'Ten Wheels For Jesus' can't be far off). I think the body count on the album is 41 people and a dog.

Paradise Studios in Woolloomooloo was booked from midday till 6 pm on a Sunday in late October 1983. Even though we had six hours booked in the studio we actually did the whole record in about four. Roger Grierson made the mistake of giving everyone involved their hundred dollars *before* we started the session and of course Tony immediately headed up the road to Kings Cross to score so that was the first two hours gone.

We finally got underway some time around 2 pm with our skinny bellies full of beer and our faces full of speed. At some point I took a moment to pause and look around; I was 18, in a studio with my favourite musicians in the world making a record! I was happy – very, very happy.

Spencer arrived a bit later. The Gun Club were touring Australia at the time and a couple of them didn't make it here so Spencer and Billy Pommer from The Johnnys were filling in. By the time he did arrive he was still going from the night before, which had been the final night of the Gun Club tour. I'd never seen anyone higher or drunker than Spencer P. Jones when he arrived that afternoon.

This was frowned upon by Kim but to tell you the truth Spencer did work very well . . . for a while. The last thing we recorded was 'Lonesome Bones'. Spencer played slide guitar on that and it's all over the place, but it's perfect for what we were aiming for. I can't imagine it any other way. Jonesy played his guitar lying flat on his back and I don't think he stood up again until we left. He finished playing 'Lonesome Bones' and passed out on the floor. There was no more he could do.

I didn't know it then but it would never be this simple and pure again.

In the end we'd done mostly first takes, and there were no other songs recorded for B-sides. There's no fat or leftovers whatsoever on *The Axeman's Jazz*. Everything got used. I think that's why that album works better than other Beasts albums. Ten-song albums are usually the best and that one's nine. The whole record is recorded as a totally live mix straight to tape. Perfect. There was no sense in recording it and then having a mixing session later and figuring it out. There was no time and money anyway.

At the time we of course had no idea that this would become such an important and influential album to so many. Today it's frequently cited as one of the most significant independent Australian albums of that era – and has ended up selling a LOT of copies both here and overseas.

This was, and still is, the purest of the Beasts' albums. Later the band started doing 13- and 15-song albums and at times heading down a few artistic dead ends. I think all those records would work better being 10-song albums or less. For that reason alone *The Axeman's Jazz* is my favourite of the Beasts' albums. It's also for me a document of one of the best days of my life.

THE AXEMAN'S JAZZ

THE BEASTS OF BOURBON / 1983

A six-hour session, this really IS all about being thrown
in the deep end. Stink or swim, I think we did both. You've
just read a whole chapter on this recording session so
there's no need to repeat all that here. I have to say, one
of my favourite parts of this album comes before a note
is even played. At the start of the record before the first
song 'Evil Ruby' you can hear the sounds of the Beasts
preparing to commence recording. Spencer says 'James' to
which James answers 'Hey? I, I don't start it', followed by
my goofy 18-year-old's chuckle. Then a decisive '1,2,3,4'
from Kim and we were away.

RECORD LABEL: *GREEEN, 1984, reissued on Red Eye, 1988*
CORE BAND MEMBERS: *Tex Perkins (vocals), Spencer P. Jones (guitar),
Kim Salmon (guitar), Boris Sujdovic (bass), James Baker (drums).*

Dad, off to war aged 19.

Me and Mum in Darwin, 1965.
Note the racially insensitive t-shirt.

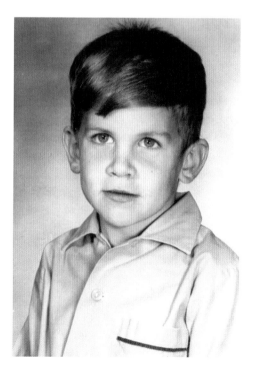

Tex Perkins. First grade, 1970.
What the fuck happened?

Me aged 14 with my
first guitar.

The Dum Dums playing in Brisbane, early 1982 (pre-'Tex Deadly' Dum Dums). That's Ian Wadley on guitar. That's me holding onto the mic stand for dear life.

Stripsearched, photographed, fingerprinted and fifty bucks bail. All this for saying the word 'fuck' in a conversation with friends.

Putting another log on the fire at Jules Normington's place in Woollahra, 1983.

There it is! The van we drove to Sydney for the first Dum Dums tour in 1982.

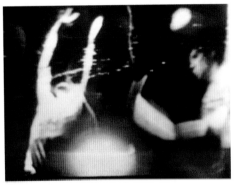

Scenes of chaos: Thug live.

Butcher Shop boys: Lachlan McLeod, Peter Hartley (on
the telly), Phil Clifford and me, circa 1988.

Tex on Big Tex. Thug always left audiences muttering 'What the fuck just happened?'

Above that's me with the Beasts at the Gunnery squat I lived in from 1988 to 1990: me, Kim, Boris, James and Spencer.
Tony and Brian are in the line-up on the right (at the back), just before we recorded *The Low Road* in 1990. At this stage we were pretty horrible but not yet fully, delightfully horrible.

Courtesy Tony Mott

The Cruel Sea, 1989. Notice my mullet, but also notice the reverse mullets on Dan, Jim and James: short at the bottom and thick at the top.

Courtesy Tony Mott

The Cruel Sea, 1991. Mullets gone, Dan still wearing the same shirt.

Kristyna took this photo the night we met in Berlin.
Inexplicably she wasn't completely repulsed.

The Beasts, 1993.

Tex, Don & Charlie, 1994.

Courtesy Tony Mott

LONDON CALLING

Sometime in late 1984 I got a letter from Kid Congo Powers.

I'd met Kid the year before when The Gun Club toured Australia. Kid just happened to have been in two of my favourite ever bands – The Cramps and The Gun Club. In the letter he told me that The Gun Club were winding up and that I should come to London as soon as possible so he and I could start a band together. And I went 'OKAY, LET'S GO' and organised a quick Beasts of Bourbon gig so I could raise the thousand dollars I'd need to buy a plane ticket to London

I was 19 and as green as snot from a leprechaun. Having never been overseas before I had no knowledge at all as to what you do when going to another country to form a rock'n'roll band. I was so naïve I figured you just jumped on a plane and got there. No one told me the last thing you say to British customs officials is 'I'm in a band'. But that's pretty much what I did and it did not go down well.

'You're goin' to be in a bund y'say?' said the man at immigration. 'Oh reeeally?' Then he asked me if I had a work permit and of course I had to say no. I didn't even know such a thing existed. I tried to explain that I didn't have a work permit at that stage as we didn't actually have a band. But we were *going* to have a band and then I guessed I'd apply for a work permit. But because we didn't have a band yet and we weren't working, I didn't have one or need one yet.

It was logic that made sense to me – but not to them.

Furthermore, I told them there was no need to worry about me because I wasn't going to go on the dole or anything like that. I wasn't going to be a burden on them or the system. I *was* going to work, but not just yet, but when I did work, I'd certainly get a work permit.

Okay?

Unsurprisingly, they weren't buying it. They told me that without a work permit they weren't letting me into the UK and that I should go and sit on that bench over there and that they'd deal with me soon. Then they started to go through my belongings and have a good look at everything.

It must be said that I wasn't really all that clever in my packing for international travel. Back at the squat I'd been living in I'd just run my arm across a table with all my things on it and swept it into a suitcase. Now there was lots of weird, stupid, slightly incriminating things in there which they started to judge me on. Suddenly there was this whole 'What do we have here?' vibe.

I spent three days in this little white room in the detention centre at Gatwick airport being interrogated for eight hours a day by all sorts of different people who kept asking me 'Do you take drugs?!' I kept saying that I *didn't* take drugs. They kept saying that my luggage and appearance *suggested I took drugs*. I kept saying *I didn't take drugs*. 'We've been reading some your "lyrics" and we think they sound like they've been written by someone on drugs.' They had nothing on me but they just didn't believe me. So I was just playing the *no, no, no, not me* game, but they weren't giving up. They could just smell something on me. Not literally. But almost.

Then it got a little more serious. They got hold of the addresses of all the people in London that I had written in my diary and sent police around to visit those places to see if those people took drugs or could confirm that I took drugs. That made me REALLY popular with the good people on whose couches I intended to crash during my stay in London.

Luckily they didn't find anything at those addresses or on me as there was nothing to find. But they still kept me there for three days. These customs officials really thought they were going to nail me with something. They thought 'this freak has got to be on drugs and he will know more people who are on drugs and we will take him down and then we'll take them ALL down'.

Obviously I was a bit of a drug taker. They knew it. I knew it. But I wasn't going to admit it even when I lost count of how many people had interrogated me. Initially they did the whole good cop–bad cop routine on me but they soon ran out of good cops. I was scared, but without any actual drugs on my person or in my suitcase I knew they couldn't really nail me for anything, so I just stayed as calm as I could and denied everything.

At one point they even had a doctor physically examine me for needle marks or any other telltale marks of drug use of any kind on my body. Nothing. At the end of each day of interrogation I was sent back to the white room in the detention centre, a small dormitory I shared with other detainees – some very sad-looking guys from an African country who didn't speak English.

Refused entry.

Eventually they confirmed they weren't going to let me into the country. They were refusing me entry to England and that was it. But they weren't sending me back to Australia either. Oh no, the way it worked was that they sent you back to the last place you were before you came to London and in my case due to connecting flights the last place was Manila.

So there I was. I had no money. My passport bore the big stamp REFUSED ENTRY and I was being deported to Manila.

Now I was basically a captive of Philippine Airlines. They didn't want to but they were forced by the aviation rules and regulations to take me to Manila – and for free.

I'd been through quite a bit by then. An initial flight of about 36 hours, then 80-odd hours at Gatwick being interrogated, and now a flight to Manila. I was a wreck. When the plane finally landed in Manila the first thing I heard was an announcement saying, 'Welcome to the Philippines where the mandatory punishment for drugs is death.'

That sent a shiver through me.

That shiver became a cold sweat when another announcement asked, 'Would Greg Perkins come to the front of the plane please?' This was before anyone was even allowed to get off the plane, or even leave their seats.

So up I go in front of everyone like I was walking to the gallows in my polka-dot shirt and these ridiculous stovepipe pants I've been wearing for four days straight, my hair like dirty black straw, incredibly thin, incredibly pale and incredibly smelly.

Quite a sight.

I'm met by some serious Filipino guys in uniform who escort me off the plane, hand me over to airport ground-staff who put me in the front seat of an airport buggy next to the driver. Then they go back into the plane and reappear a few minutes later with two guys in business suits. The suits jump in the back seat and we all head off on this long ride through Manila airport towards the unknown.

As we get towards the end of one of the many extremely long concourses I see a crowd of people gathered, and as we get closer, I can see that they're all looking at us. A lot of them are photographers and as we get to them they all start taking pictures. Then there's this whole presentation – a welcoming ceremony. And it's clearly not for me. Turns out the two guys in suits are German diplomats come to sign some important trade deal or something and I'm caught up in the middle of it all. I like to imagine we all made the front page of the *Manila Gazette*.

After the press call and welcoming ceremony, the suits went to their plush hotel and I lived in the transit lounge of Manila airport for the next 48 hours, sleeping on the floor with only a series of security guards to keep me company. I had to try to organise for someone in Australia to buy a ticket home for me. But this was in the mid-'80s. There was no email or mobile phones or instant cash transfers.

I rang James Baker, and I think Roger Grierson also might have helped stump up the funds. This was my family in Sydney and we all lived by the credo that *we take care of our own*. It impressed me no end that people thought enough of me to include me in that thinking. And it was also good to have people back there who had their shit together enough to get a thousand dollars together pretty fast to get me home.

Eventually I arrived back in Australia on a Thursday, having left the Thursday before . . . and without actually ever having arrived anywhere.

ADELAIDE VIA AMSTERDAM

After being refused entry to England the first time and after going through the hell I did, I'm still amazed that neither I, nor Kid Congo and the rest of the Americans in London were deterred.

We were all still determined to get me to London to begin work on our new band together.

By now the band had a name, THE FUR BIBLE, which sounded both strangely sexual and blasphemous at the same time. I think it came from an actual expensive fur catalogue ... but maybe not.

A new plan is hatched! This time I will fly to Amsterdam, meet Kid and spend a few weeks there, deliberately destroy my passport, (by putting in a washing machine) get a fresh (temporary) one *without* the words REFUSED ENTRY stamped inside it, and then catch a bus that will cross the Channel in a ferry and then through to London. It's a plan. (At least this time there is a plan.)

And this time I'll do it differently.

When I flew I made sure I didn't wear anything that might draw attention to me. I wore clothes totally different to what I would normally and combed my hair over and flattened it to my head as much as it could be.

I realise now that in my attempt to look 'straight', the effect was more like a guy that had just got out of jail or a young thug's day-in-court clobber. Which is probably why, out of around 300 people who walked through customs, they chose me to do a full bag and body search on.

Now I'd been through this before very recently so I knew the drill, but these guys were next level. As soon as the door closed on the little white room they started shouting at me:

'YOU'RE A DRUG ADDICT – ADMIT IT!'

Seriously, in all the interrogations I went through at Gatwick nobody had reached this level of fury and accusation so quickly! These Dutch guys were acting like they really wanted to hurt me. *They were furious.*

'STAND THERE. TAKE YOUR CLOTHES OFF.'

After they looked into my anus, I stood there naked for the rest of the 'interview'.

'YOUR CLOTHES STINK,' they sneered. 'YOU'RE DIS-GUSTING.'

I kid you not, these fellas were born 50 years too late, if you know what I mean.

They looked through everything in my luggage, which this time had a lot less incriminating stuff. And they spent quite a bit of time looking through my photo album, pointing and laughing and speaking to each other in Dutch.

Then suddenly one of them said, 'You're free to go, get out.'

'Okay . . . no apology?'

'What for?'

On reflection, I feel sorry for those chaps. I mean who brings drugs INTO Amsterdam from Australia? They must've been bored out of their minds. Desperate to nab someone, anyone, for anything. There's probably not a lot going on during their shift. So when they get even a sniff they're absolutely rabid.

Eventually I got out of there and into Amsterdam. Met up with Kid Congo and had an awesome two weeks planning our next move and getting to know each other. I've been fortunate to fall in with a lot of great people along my way through life. Kid is one the best. We shared our ideas and were very excited about what we were about to do together.

Eventually I successfully made my way over to London, where I started this band with Kid and Patricia Morrison who'd both recently left The Gun Club.

It was *terrible*.

By then we're smack bang in 1985 and it's all post punk, which was okay, but what was really fashionable at the time was goth. Some of those bands were okay, but when I actually saw it up close in London, as opposed to the filtered version we saw in Australia, I saw how much of a monoculture fashion thing it was.

I thought, *Wow, this is . . . kinda boring.*

Bands like The Birthday Party were really exciting back in 1981 and 1982 but by the time 1985 came along that whole Nick Cave thing was really stale and pompous to a lot of us. And that whole goth thing with lots of makeup? Sisters Of Mercy and those bands? It was just horrible.

The band Kid and Patricia were putting together was heading towards being a bit London and a bit goth and a bit shit. I didn't dig it at all so I stuck it out for a few months and then skulked back to Australia.

By the time I returned home my girlfriend Hazel had moved back to her home city of Adelaide, so I followed suit. Yes that's right I moved TO Adelaide. I needed somewhere out of the way to recuperate and re-think my position, and Madelaide was perfect. The people I hung out with there had a more of an *art punk* attitude. They were all messy and there was lots of all kinds of creativity. Most people wore freaky clothes, not so much of the typical punk rock garb. They were

Me and Kid Congo.

dirty and colourful. Hazel was living with a couple known as Jude and Justine. Jude was loud and eccentric and Justine opened my eyes to the world of lo fi home recordings

For me this was a tiny but new and interesting subculture. The flagship of this scene were the very noisy and very funny Purple Vulture Shit.

Lead 'singer' Toe (real name Chris Cashel) had what I think were the finest lyrics around:

> *I'm going to get married to a Ringworm one day.'*
> *'And we'll live up a celebrities arse . . .*
> *Hole, eating toilet paper.*

With songs like that and a name like theirs, Purple Vulture Shit were an important influence in terms of just how unmusical you can be and still have something interesting to put onstage.

A lot of people were totally and absolutely appalled by Purple Vulture Shit, but to me the ineptitude of the players didn't matter at all, just so long as you weren't shy about it.

If you laid into it and had a go, that was all that mattered. There's nothing worse than someone who's not very good at something being shy and coy and frightened about it.

NO APOLOGIES.

All those crazy bands I met during this two- or three-year period in Adelaide – Purple Vulture Shit, Sunday School, Manic Opera, The Plungers, The Stink Pots – were noisy, messy and funny with names guaranteed to upset someone somewhere.

There was no thought of longevity or of this particular band having any sort of a career. No one thought of anything beyond doing a gig, having some fun and making a mess.

It was in Adelaide that I formed what became one of my favourite and most enduring ensembles: The Bumhead Orchestra.

The first time we stumbled across the idea there were four of us in the room. Dave Taskas (the bass player from Grong Grong), Justin and Lachlan McLeod. We were calling it a rehearsal but we had nothing – no songs, no idea. So at some stage I started *conducting* the band.

At its most basic, my conducting style was GO and STOP. But at its most complex I resembled a highly emotional traffic cop. There were crescendos, up and down sweeps of the hand for louder/softer and various solos. It was a *controlled cacophony*.

The beauty of The Bumhead Orchestra was that there were so many ways it could go. It wasn't always noise. It could very much be an orchestrated jam. I could point to the drummer and he'd start playing a beat. Then I might build the sound fairly conventionally and point to the bass, then violin, organ, slide whistle, tuba, theremin, trumpet, and then a single ding of the triangle.

You getting a picture here?

It's . . . flexible. Every member of the orchestra can approach it as very high brow or really low brow. And the key to it? At my signal, the orchestra must be ready to emit sound at any moment, with a split-second's warning. For me as conductor that means being completely committed to physically embodying the music's intent, desperately attempting to describe what I want with only my body and a small stick. Usually a chopstick.

After its Adelaide inception, The Bumhead Orchestra consisted of me getting as many people onstage as possible with as many different instruments as possible – preferably instruments they were not very familiar with but could make some sort of sound with.

A typical Bumhead performance could stretch to about 20 minutes but I believe in brevity and directness when it comes to noise (and The Bumhead Orchestra was *very* noisy) so usually a performance was included on a mixed-bill night. That was the ideal because then at the end of the night every band member could gather together as The Bumhead Orchestra.

The Bumhead thing probably peaked on the 2006 Big Day Out. The Beasts Of Bourbon were on the tour that year and so promoter Ken West asked me if I wouldn't mind doing the Bumhead Orchestra as well. Ken was essentially a businessman but he loved all that silly, arty stuff and the Lily Pad, where the weird cabaret stuff and arty off-the-wall elements happened, was really where his heart was at. A dude called Duck Pond and all those goofy people had free reign over the place so the Bumheads fit right in.

Among the many interesting characters I met from Adelaide was

Thug live at ... I have no idea. That's me on top of 'Big Tex' (10 foot tall), wrapped in plastic and bound in masking tape.

another fella named Tex. Like me he'd been given the nickname and it had stuck. So when we started hanging around in the same group of friends it became necessary to differentiate between us. He became known as 'Big Tex', which suited him because he was about 6 foot 7. Luckily I didn't become known as 'Little Tex' (after all I was almost 6 foot 4). His real name was Chris Tunks, and his little brother played rugby league for Australia.

Big Tex was big but he was also one of the gentlest souls I've ever met. He was a very wise and spiritual person. Having been to India many times, Big Tex had a bit of a guru vibe. I often looked to him if I needed advice. I felt safe around him and not many people have ever made me feel like that.

Big Tex and I played together in Toilet Duck, but he was also a kind of performance artist in Thug. Dressed as an Oxford street leather man Big Tex would randomly come on stage and push one of us over and then storm off again. We would listen to and discuss all sorts of music but importantly Tex was the only person in our scene that would openly admit to listening to not just crazy noisy weird stuff but traditional things like the early Rolling Stones.

I'd loved the Stones album *Sticky Fingers* earlier in my life but hadn't bothered lending an ear for a few years at that point. It was the mid-'80s for fuck's sake and the Stones were awful then. So I initially resisted the big fella's influence on this. But then one day I was at his flat and he played me the soundtrack to the film *Performance*, starring Mick Jagger.

Released in 1970 and produced by Jack Nitzsche, *Performance* is a collection and a collision of blues, rock, electronic, beat poetry, orchestral and Indian folk music. Randy Newman, Ry Cooder, Mick Jagger and The Last Poets all make appearances on this wild ride of an album.

Big Tex and *Performance* showed me a way out of the avant-garde and back to the desert and the swamp I'd come from. Ry Cooder was a major component in all this. On this soundtrack you hear him play Indian tabla, and on slide guitar an early version of 'Dark Is The Night', which he later used for the *Paris, Texas* soundtrack. It taught me great soundtracks complement and enhance their accompanying films but the greatest soundtracks of all make the film itself unnecessary and create a world of their own.

Fuelled by such powerful art, music and bonhomie, this very intense and creative period had nothing to do with furthering my career in music. Looking back it was actually burning bridges in terms of professionalism, progression and knowledge and developing skills in business. Those two years in London via Amsterdam and ultimately Adelaide were all about rejecting everything and making a mess. A loud, funny colourful mess.

Everything that London wasn't.

THUG

Peter Read was one of the most unique individuals I have ever met.

I dare say a lot of people would say the same thing. He was one of those people who had their very own idiosyncrasies, aesthetic and sense of humour. He had a hilarious habit of making sounds. Verbal outbursts indicating an emotion of some kind. Let me try to explain.

Let's start with *eow*. This would be blurted out in a short sharp stab: *EOW!*

This was a sound of approval and excitement. There may be just one, or a short series of them – *eow eow eow*. It could be used to express how delicious he thought his meal was, how pretty a girl was or how much he liked a band.

A very similar 'word' was used to express disappointment.

Eeeooow was basically an elongated *eow* delivered with a kind of sneer.

These were the big two, but there were many more. *Rrrabadee, hoinggg,* and *weeeee* were used often, but the word he would use the most was PENIS. He loved saying the word PENIS. And would hilariously drop it in to any conversation at any time. To a cab driver:

'Can you take us to the corner of Oxford Street and Penis, please driver?'

'Excuse me?'

'The corner of Oxford Street and Bourke Street, please?'

Or it may be blurted out in a quiet corner store. PENIS! There were other Tourette's-like outbursts that would become standards and they were widely repeated. One night we were in someone's car and Peter got excited and shouted:

'SPASTIC WEE WEE WETTY BOTTOM!'

Everyone in the car roared with laughter. This only encouraged Peter to go further and further.

Peter was a nudist, and when he was nude was when he made the most sounds.

'*Rrrabadeee eow eow eow!!!*'

But Peter was also extremely talented. He was a natural musician

Peter Read, 1987.

who was trained in nothing but who could make any instrument speak for him in a unique way. He had a totally original musical angle.

Peter's flatmate Dave had an addiction to collecting and amassing electronic equipment . . . that he then never used. But we would. All the drum machines, effects and samplers we used during these years, Peter would push beyond their assumed limits. Most of this equipment was in the very top floor flat of the Riverina apartments that Peter and Dave shared on Palmer Street, Darlinghurst. When I returned to Sydney from Adelaide, that's where we made so much of this music.

Peter was incredibly talented but he was also an incredibly difficult individual. I always saw the potential in what he did. I was very enthusiastic and would want to bring all these ideas out of the bedroom and try to make something of them, but he was always reluctant to do that and strangely unbelieving of his own music's worth. Peter always had to be dragged along. It drove me crazy and I lost it with him quite a few times.

After using his gear on some initial recordings in Peter's home studio, I wanted to take it to the stage, so around 1987 Peter and I formed Thug.

With the help of Lachlan McLeod and others, Thug became one of Sydney's most unconventional, confronting but ultimately ridiculous live acts. Once, we discovered a small trampoline and gym mats backstage at a hall we were playing and dragged them out to do our set, leaping through the air recklessly, somersaulting on and off stage.

Thug's live sets would last 20–25 minutes at the most but could feature a dancing leather man, a fire-breathing unicyclist, homemade junk robots, guerrilla acrobatics, bizarre malfunctioning electronic equipment and – at one performance – an entire audience showered in flour (it was a 'goth' club where everyone wore black, so we thought . . .).

We always left the audience with a 'what the fuck just happened?' kind of feeling.

Each Thug gig would end with all the members mock-brawling among themselves. Audience members also would participate from time to time and of course sometimes it would get out of hand. During one such 'mock brawl', I ended up with a gaping hole in my thigh requiring stitches after landing on a broken glass someone had thrown onto the stage.

Black Eye bruisers, Sydney, 1987. Stu Spasm, Lachlan McLeod, Peter Read and Perko.

At our *BROKEN ROBOT* show at the gunnery squat, we had the whole stage draped with rolls of bubble wrap. Donato, our horn-playing fire-breathing unicyclist, accidentally set the stage floor alight. I'm sure the most frightening and entertaining thing for the audience that night would have been watching us frantically running about stomping out the flames.

Thug was all about sounds – some would call it noise. Ugly sounds, beautiful sounds, stupid sounds, all kinds of sounds. Ninety-nine per cent of Thug's recordings were achieved by letting the tape roll and just playing. Sometimes not even playing, just allowing sound *to occur.*

Thug, along with Lubricated Goat and Kim Salmon & The Surrealists spearheaded this understandably overlooked and underrated era of Australian music. As obscure as it all was the 'Blackeye' scene has been mythologised in the underground for many years.

But of course Thug are best remembered for the song 'Dad', or 'Fuck your Dad' as it was better known.

> *Alone at home with your father*
> *He's good looking*
> *Do it now*
> *Fuck your Dad.*

People in the already established electronic/experimental scene didn't quite know how to take us. Once again it was the age old questions, 'Are you taking the piss?'; 'Are you serious?'

We were into *extremities*. If you listen to some of our records – *Mechanical Ape* or *Electric Woolly Mammoth* you'll hear some frighteningly rude noise but it's followed by some very gentle melodic music. Thug albums were like channel-surfing through a schizophrenic's multiple-personality disorders. But it was all anchored by humour. We'd always be laughing when we created the sounds of Thug.

Obviously we weren't doing anything for commercial reasons but the 'Fuck Your Dad' single was a real statement back then. The single was just called 'Dad' and the B-side was 'Thug'. Two songs on a piece of plastic. And bugger me, it made number one on the Sydney independent music charts!

It must have sold close to 100 copies that week . . . okay, maybe 50.

After Thug, Peter went on to make a lot of really interesting, funny, strange and exciting bedroom music. But he never released anything much again. I often visited him after he moved to Melbourne and always saw his potential but as more time went by Peter's idiosyncrasies didn't stay as cute and funny as they once had been. His verbal acrobatics were replaced by mumblings, rapid mood swings and crippling self-doubt followed by uncontrollable

Lachlan McLeod would set his hair on fire quite regularly.

laughing that went way past the point of enjoyment. It was as if Peter was locked in a cycle of laughter he couldn't break out of. But his music remained delightfully out there and I loved him for it.

Peter dying in August 2016 wasn't a shock, I knew he was sick. As far as I know he didn't take any treatment for his liver cancer, he let it take its course over a period of 18 months. Then, instead of grasping for a few extra months through chemotherapy, at a point of his choosing he decided he'd had enough.

Peter owned his disease *and* his death.

I salute you, Peter Read. You'll never be replaced.

Peter.

MECHANICAL APE

THUG / 1987

A ridiculous mess of noise and beauty. This album startled
and confused many that heard it, but is much loved by a
small group of weirdos around the world. It was recorded
in Peter Read's bedroom on a Fostex 4-track cassette
recorder over many days of marijuana and Coopers Ale.
Not many songs, but a lot of sounds that – listening to it
now – I can't remember how we achieved.

RECORD LABEL: *Black Eye*
CORE BAND MEMBERS: *Tex Perkins (vocals), Peter Read, Donato Rosella
(didgeridoo/saxophone).*

ELECTRIC WOOLLY MAMMOTH

THUG / 1988

The follow up to *Mechanical Ape*, this album is a little more conventional as it has a few 'songs' with 'words', even if they are things like 'penis, penis, penis bosom bosom arsehole'. Here, Peter's unique form of Tourette's found full voice. Squelching undanceable 'dance' music, slabs of brown noise and delicate ambient sample loops make for an interesting ride through this second and final Thug album.

RECORD LABEL: *Black Eye*
CORE BAND MEMBERS: *Tex Perkins (vocals), Peter Read, Donato Rosella (didgeridoo/saxophone), Lachlan McLeod (guitar).*

RED EYE BLACK EYE

In Sydney in the mid-'80s, we used to make up bands all the time.

If there were three people in a room together you'd be a band. We'd form a band for one night – and then you'd make a band with someone else. Just as in Adelaide, there was no thought of anyone having any sort of a career. No one thought of anything beyond having some fun, making a mess and taking the piss.

Bands were everywhere and there were still places you could play. I was in The Bush Oysters, Thug, The Poofters, Toilet Duck, The Bumhead Orchestra, The Furry Men of the North, Hot Property and The Boilers, just to name a few.

But thank fuck for John Foy and Red Eye/ Black Eye Records.

I'd first met John around 1983. I had moved into Phantom Records founder Jules Normington's place in Queen Street,

Woollahra. I was 17 and Jules was probably nearly 30 but for some reason he took a shine to me and took me under his wing. Woollahra was full of well-heeled Eastern Suburbs types, but when it came to me and Jules, I guess there were exceptions.

My contribution to Jules's home was that I washed the dishes. For that chore I got free board and access to the best record collection I have ever seen. Jules specialised in '60s and '70s garage rock. Anything you can think of from that era? He had the original pressings. Those Nuggets compilations? He had every track as a single. I spent months digesting Jules's vinyl goldmine, washing dishes and sleeping in the shed.

Dancing on the roof of Jules Normington's place 1983 in our pyjamas.

John Foy was living next door designing and screen-printing posters for bands on Jules's Phantom label when he decided to start his own label, Red Eye Records, borrowing the name from the record shop he worked in at the time. The first thing he did was release a single by James Baker under the name the James Baker Experience. This was not long after James had been fired from the Hoodoo Gurus. The A-side of this single was a song called 'Born to Be Punched' which everyone – including James – thought was about Gurus lead singer Dave Faulkner. The other side was a ragged version of The Troggs song 'I Can't Control Myself'.

I was actually part of the James Baker Experience – along with Roddie Ray'Da and Stu Spasm. I played bass . . . I think.

After *The Axeman's Jazz*, Roger Grierson and Stuart Coupe's label, G.R.E.E.N, stopped releasing things. Their deal with Big Time Records – a label run by this guy called Fred Bestall who'd made some serious money managing Air Supply – had gone arse-up. So now, with Roger caught up managing The Johnnys and Stuart managing Paul Kelly between writing gigs, John Foy approached me about re-releasing *The Axeman's Jazz* on Red Eye.

None of the Beasts had made any money on the initial *Axeman's* release. Big Time Records had declared bankruptcy before paying us any royalties. But when we eventually went to Europe to play, EVERYONE had a copy of that album so it certainly got around. Even so, no one really owned it so there was no legality around Red Eye reissuing the record and Roger and Stuart were happy for us to have it.

After the *Axeman's* re-issue, Red Eye released a Salamander Jim EP, *Lorne Green Shares His Precious Fluids*.

Salamander Jim was a minimalist rockabilly swamp outfit I'd formed with Kim Salmon before he left for London. By the time we recorded *Lorne*, the band included Martin Bland from Zulu Rattle, Lubricated Goat's Stu Spasm and Broken Hill boy Lachlan McLeod, with Ewan Cameron from Whore's Manure on saxophone.

During the period I was in London and then licking my wounds in Adelaide, John Foy had started working in the indie-pop-rock area with the various Kilbeys – Russell with the Crystal set, John with the Baghavad Guitars and Steve who was doing all this stuff outside The Church.

One night Thug and a few other 'acts' played at a pub in Kings Cross and John Foy turned up for a look. The usual tornado of noise, mess, colour, and stupidity tore through the room for our customary 20-minute set, but that was enough for John. He was in love and decided on the spot that the world needed to hear Thug unleashed upon the cultural landscape.

But by now Red Eye was an indie pop label and to release bands like Real Fucking Idiots and Purple Vulture Shit on *that* label just wouldn't do, so the idea came to form another label. We wanted to call it Brown Eye but John Foy preferred Black Eye and in the next few years he made it the launchpad for a series of compilations that brought together the wildest, weirdest and funniest 'acts' around: Thug, Lubricated Goat, Grong Grong, Toe, Moist, No More Bandicoots and Box The Jesuit all coexisted in a stew of filthy experimental rock and absurdist toilet humour. It was like the *whole scene* had Tourette's.

During the Black Eye period we used various pubs around Sydney as our bomb sites for mixed-bill performances, but the Petersham Inn on Parramatta Road became Black Eye head-quarters. Duncan Stewart, who ran the pub, loved us. And we loved him. Duncan was about 6 foot 5 and about 50 years old, but he had a boyish enthusiasm for our mischief and he basic-ally gave us license to do anything we wanted in his hotel.

Anything. Anytime. Dangerous words for people like me and my friends.

On any given night we brought together the most bizarre and unusual things we could. But by way of thanks to Duncan, we also hosted frequent shows by Hot Property, a ridiculous covers band that would play (what we thought) were the most awful hits of the '70s and '80s. Duncan loved it.

Our audience were the weirdos that other weirdos thought were too weird. People with names like Drip Tray and Fish Pump. On any given night Thug, or Lubricated Goat, maybe Box The Jesuit, or the Space Juniors, or No More Bandicoots or Egg n Burgers, Toilet Duck or The Poofters or Whores Manure would play. Sometimes we'd put on Stu Spasm's one-man terror cabaret act Chicken Holder, or a performance group we knew called Butchered Babies. Whatever we felt like doing Duncan would run with, and happily. Gleefully.

Sometimes the performances weren't even bands. Or people.

I had this massive stereo at my place, a home entertainment unit which contained a television, a turntable and a radio in the one unit. It was built in the late 1950s I'd guess. There was no aerial so it wouldn't actually pick up the television signal and there'd be no pictures or anything, but when the valves in the thing heated up it would send a frequency through the radio which was like a theremin, which I could manipulate by touching different parts of the unit's cabinet. This random, oscillating but not repetitive, sound would go all over the place and get wilder and wilder, plus there would be corresponding static on the television flashing strange patterns echoing the sounds. I'd just sit in front of it captivated.

Now, I realise that may not sound like everybody's cup of pee, but I loved it and thought this unique experience should be shared on the stage.

I called it The Unit and on the night of its debut performance I put the Thug single 'Dad'/'Thug' on the turntable at a slower speed with a pencil blu-tacked to the arm and the side of the deck so that the needle would stick in one spot on the record. Grinding loops of thick sludge roared from the speakers. When I tired of each loop I would briefly come on stage, kick the unit to make the needle jump and create a different loop, and then exit again stage left.

Inspired partly by Peter Read, who was always looking for the 'wrong' way to do things, I developed a knack for rebirthing broken things. I found all sorts of bizarrely malfunctioning electronic equipment on hard rubbish nights in those days. I found a 'ghetto blaster' that completely freaked out with screaming feedback when plugged in – I would strap it to my body with gaffer tape for Thug performances and occasionally thrust a mike into it. These were items broken in a conventional sense but, in the context of Thug, they became wonderful self-generating noise machines.

One of the greatest ideas we had was to give away free beer to anyone who was nude. Duncan LOVED it. (Of course he did.)

The idea was simple. If you went to the Petersham Inn completely naked you'd receive a free beer. Nothing complicated about that. Sure enough, maybe 100 people turned up and many of them were nude. Totally nude. Just as everyone had a different approach to performance, everyone had a different approach to being nude. Some chose to wear their clothes into the pub and then disrobe to get their free beer and then they'd get dressed again. They would do this many times during the course of the evening. Others just stayed nude all night.

Let me tell you, it wasn't sexy. It was just weird and really funny. And that's exactly the atmosphere we were after.

In fact nudity was rife in this era. Take, for example, No More Bandicoots. Whenever they played at the Petersham Inn or anywhere else they'd have some sort of theme to that night's show. Once they all dressed as pirates and made the front of the stage into a pirate ship with cardboard and paint. It was really like a punk rock school play. Other nights they'd be completely nude and covered in shaving cream.

The greatest nudist of all was Peter Read. Pete might be at his home (or someone else's) then disappear briefly. Next thing you knew he'd reappear completely nude – and just carry on as if he wasn't.

There were many nude adventures with Pete. One night we invented Nude Piggyback Punch Ball – two In conjunction with Duncan. The first Annual Sausage Meet, 1987.

nude men piggybacking two other nude men while battling to punch a football suspended on a string from the ceiling in the middle of the room. We played it, and filmed it.

Eventually the infamy of Stu Spasm's nude disco led to a nude performance by Lubricated Goat on Andrew Denton's late night ABC show *Blah Blah Blah*.

Weirdly, the members of Lubricated Goat at the time refused to do the nude thing, (*Australia, you don't know how lucky you are*) so Stuart was forced to beg Peter Hartley, who he had recently sacked from the band, to come back just to be nude on TV. Peter was quite a physically attractive young man so that was a good choice. And Peter Read, who wasn't actually in Lubricated Goat, was also recruited to play because of his complete and total willingness to go nude.

The performance drew widespread outrage of course, mainly because it was on the national broadcaster ABC. 'Government funded filth!' cried Alan Jones. The Goat squeezed all they could out of their time in the media storm. After that no one got nude anymore. The bubble had burst and nude went mainstream. It was time to get dressed and move on.

This era didn't just bring nudity. It brought the noise.

The first compilation issued on Black Eye was *Waste Sausage*. We had considered calling it *Ripper 86* as a homage to those Ripper compilations in the 1970s. On the cover of each of the Rippers was a picture of a woman's bottom in a pair of shorts ripped to the waist exposing a lot of lady rump.

Using all that vacant real estate, the Rippers wrote the track list right there on the lady's bum. Black Eye's *Ripper 86* was going to have Stu Spasm's bottom on the cover but strangely Foy didn't buy into the concept of a really hairy man's arse as the cover of the album. We did talk him into putting two naked men playing pool on the back cover.

A second compilation, *Leather Donut*, was released in '88. But by then the bills were starting to roll in for John.

From the start John was all about creating things rather than making money. But that aesthetic can't last forever. We'd had our fun and now it was time to pay the piper. Black Eye folded quickly with a few releases left in the pipeline, one being the legendary third compilation *Hairy Biscuit*.

That's always the case with record labels. I've never blamed anyone – especially an independent record label – for lack of sales. Essentially I had the philosophy that if it's good, somehow people will hear it and that side of things will take care of itself. (I was wrong of course.)

Black Eye boys on Cleveland street, Sydney, 1987.

Eventually John did a deal with PolyGram which became Universal. For Red Eye, not Black eye. It was all over for Black eye. I think he was happy to do it, but once he had the big boys on board, John slowly became less essential. The '80s were giving way to the '90s and the new era was all about the corporates buying in – capitalising on the independents and their ability to sell records to their audiences. They'd offer to do a deal and distribute the label, promising to make things much bigger – and inevitably the people who'd started those labels became unnecessary.

But without people like John Foy a lot of things just wouldn't have happened.

John Foy and me, Queen st, 1983.

LORNE GREEN SHARES HIS PRECIOUS FLUIDS

SALAMANDER JIM / 1985

Salamander Jim was a band Kim Salmon and I threw together for a few months – until he left for England. When he did, I carried on for a while with a new line-up. Stu Spasm, Lachlan McLeod and Martin Bland were unique players but this band never really came together, decided what it wanted to do and nailed it. This record's not great but at least it's got a great cover.

RECORD LABEL: *Red Eye*
CORE BAND MEMBERS: *Tex Perkins (vocals), Lachlan McLeod (guitar), Stu Spasm (guitar), Martin Bland (drums).*

WASTE SAUSAGE and LEATHER DONUT

BLACK EYE COMPILATIONS / 1986 and 1987

Waste Sausage is the first and the best of these two compilations of bands from the freak scenes of mid-'80s Australia. I contributed to tracks by Thug, The Bush Oysters and The Poofters on *Waste Sausage* and Salamander Jim, Minced Meat and The Furry Men of the North on *Leather Donut*. Grong Grong's 'Japanese Train Driver' is ferocious; Lubricated Goat's 'Jason The Unpopular' is also a killer track. Other tracks have a 'I guess you had to be there' vibe, but ALL of them sound like grubby young people having a lot of fun.

RECORD LABEL: *Black Eye*
CORE BAND MEMBERS: *A compilation of bands.*

HARD FOR YOU EP

THE BUTCHER SHOP / 1988

Spencer Jones and Kid Congo decided to make a quick
record when Kid was out here touring with The Bad
Seeds. They asked me, Billy Pommer and Phil Clifford to
join in. Spencer suggested we rerecord 'The World's Got
Everything In It', a tune he and I had recorded as a duo
called Minced Meat, but I thought something less comical
was appropriate. I wrote all three of the songs on the EP,
including the first version of the double entendre revenge
sludge classic 'Hard For You', the night before the session;
or was it the day of the recording? (It was a midnight till
dawn session with Tony Cohen.)

RECORD LABEL: *Black Eye*
CORE BAND MEMBERS: *Tex Perkins (vocals), Spencer P. Jones (guitar),
Kid Congo Powers (guitar), Billy Pommer (drums), Phillip Clifford (bass).*

SOUR MASH

THE BEASTS OF BOURBON / 1988

Finally tiring of making only bodily noises for the last few years I started writing 'rock' songs again and needed a rock band to play them. Kim Salmon and Boris Sujdovic were back in Australia, so the Beasts were reborn. A mixed bag, *Sour Mash* took two days for Phil Punch to record and mix. This is the first of a series of albums I made that would've been better with less songs. When a 13-song vinyl was released in a CD format it would often have B-sides attached as an extra incentive for buyers, and the album became a sprawling 15-song odyssey. Looking back now, a 10-song version would've had a greater impact. Led Zeppelin and the Stones knew this very well.

RECORD LABEL: *Red Eye*
CORE BAND MEMBERS: *Tex Perkins (vocals), Spencer P. Jones (guitar), Kim Salmon (guitar), Boris Sujdovic (bass), James Baker (drums).*

PUMP ACTION

THE BUTCHER SHOP / 1989

Once again I returned to Phil Punch for another two-day session. This time I was playing loud electric guitar, and this is the first album where I wrote all the songs. Actually maybe it's a precursor to *The Ape* where I also play electric guitar and wrote all the songs – 24 years later. It's pretty good, and stands up almost 30 years later thanks to the help of Pete Hartley, Lachlan McLeod and Phil Clifford.

RECORD LABEL: *Black Eye*
CORE BAND MEMBERS: *Tex Perkins (vocals), Pete Hartley (drums), Lachlan McLeod (guitar synth), Phillip Clifford (bass).*

LEGENDARY STARDUST COWBOYS

The Legendary Stardust Cowboy (or The Ledge as some people refer to him) was responsible for what was — and probably is still — known as The World's Worst Record.

It was a song called 'Paralyzed' and it's out there. An absolute car crash of a song. Screaming, hollering and yodelling over insane drum and bugle soloing. I loved it. Apparently The Ledge was also the guy that inspired David Bowie to use the Stardust bit in his Ziggy Stardust & The Spiders From Mars name. But that's really neither here nor there.

In 1985 a guy called Keith Glass, who ran one of Australia's first import record shops, and the Missing Link label toured The Ledge out here. (The Ledge's real name is actually Norman Carl Odam in case you were wondering.) He came to Australia with just his manager, Jim Yanaway, so Keith had to assemble two backing bands for him. He only played Sydney and

Melbourne so I guess it made economic sense to get a band in each city.

In Melbourne it was the Corpse Grinders, minus their singer Bonehead. They also backed The Ledge on a fairly hysterical performance on *Hey Hey It's Saturday* which you can see on YouTube.

In Sydney the band was me on bass, Lachlan McLeod and Spencer on guitars and James Baker on drums. Now that's a band – of sorts.

The show was at the Graphic Arts Club in Regent Street in the city and we did just one rehearsal. By that stage he had an album out that we'd had a good listen to. I won't say I was disappointed by it, but it was certainly a bit straighter than 'Paralyzed', a little bit more organised and conventional, but still hilarious and ridiculous.

Now, how do I put this? I'm not saying that Norman was mentally challenged. But he did have . . . issues. I heard a great story that one day in Melbourne he went out walking without telling anyone and his manager freaked out. 'Why did you let him go walking?! He won't come back! He can't turn corners!' Apparently he only walked in ONE direction. Couldn't, or least didn't, turn corners. A search party was sent out to find him and bring him back. Luckily someone saw him heading north. Sure enough, five kilometres down the road, there was Norman, heading north. That sort of stuff.

The Ledge was also one of those guys who only really functions as his character and stage persona when he's dressed up in his garb. A bit like Superman really. Norman put on his cowboy outfit – chaps, hat, the whole bit – and became the Legendary Stardust Cowboy. I think he preferred that to being Norman.

He drank constantly – Diet Pepsi. He had these HUGE bottles of it with him at all times.

On the night of the gig he was asleep backstage in a sitting position minutes before we went onstage.

We played this wonderful, shambolic show where Norman jumped around ranting and singing and blasting his bugle. Did I mention that his main instrument was the bugle? He threw paper plates that he had drawn a picture of himself in a UFO on, like frisbees, into the audience throughout the night.

I think our version was pretty true to Norman's style. I'm sure the Corpse Grinders did a good job at the Melbourne show but I suspect they played it straighter. I don't know that they knew how to play badly – but we certainly did. We were a very long way from conventionally structured and we embraced The Ledge's vision, if you can all it that, in that undisciplined free-form kind of way.

Outside of rehearsal and the gig I didn't spend much time around The Ledge. Jim ruffled him around like a protected species. Which he was – a unique specimen that needed special attention. As soon as the show was finished they were out of there.

He was out there and *out of there.*

Another one of the many weirdos I found myself mixed up with was P.J. Proby, an American pop singer who had been big in England for a moment in the 1960s.

He had a few hits – 'Hold Me' and 'Maria' – but not many more and I think at one stage he did some recording with The New Yardbirds who went on to become Led Zeppelin. P.J.'s other claim to fame was that he'd split his pants on stage a couple of times. That caused an uproar so then it became his schtick:

he ripped his trousers at every show until he was virtually banned in Britain.

Proby was also apparently used for demoing tunes that publishers and songwriters hoped Elvis Presley would record. These people would get their songs to Proby and he would sing them aping Elvis's style – then they'd be sent to Elvis who would ape Proby aping him when he recorded the song.

Anyway, from all that, you might be getting the idea that P.J. Proby was an unlikely contender for an Australian tour in the late '80s. But it happened and I found myself caught up in it.

Clyde Bramley had left the Hoodoo Gurus and, in a stroke of genius, decided to be a concert promoter. For some reason he thought that it was a great idea to bring P.J. Proby to Australia for a tour. *What was he thinking?* I wasn't directly involved but I knew people who knew people who were, so I kept hearing things – the decision to do it, the rehearsals etc – right up to the fateful and now legendary gig at the Paddington RSL.

It was a bizarre night. P.J. entered stage left wearing a kind of Daniel Boone outfit and sporting a grey-haired pageboy haircut and goatee. Everyone found out after it was too late that P.J. would get himself to a level of drunkenness that was a kind of madness. He'd try to start a song and it would be impossible for him. There's be all sorts of mumbling and then some bizarre, off-the-wall demented rant. It was all VERY dramatic.

Proby was always into the whole theatrical drama of the thing. I think at one point there were tears. And it IS really dramatic because he's REALLY FUCKED UP. I was in the audience and it was a case of everyone looking at each other and going 'What the fuck is happening?' I remember him taking what seemed like 20 minutes just to get this one song started.

'I'b jusht medda girl named Maria . . . MA . . . RI . . . AAAAA, ooooh.' And then he'd be briefly catatonic, frozen in a moment, mouth open, gaping wide.

And of course there's poor Clyde on bass in the background watching it all disintegrate in front of him.

There were a couple of hundred people there, in a room that could hold about a thousand or so. I saw people like Harry Dean Stanton in there around the same time and it was jammed tight, but not for P.J.. I mean, it had to be explained to me who P.J. Proby was – that he was a minor teen idol pop singer from the '60s who had a wardrobe malfunction routine. I'm guessing that if I'd never heard of him then I wasn't the only one.

Clyde and his promoting partner had P.J. staying at a shitty hotel on Campbell Parade in Bondi. So Spencer had met P.J. and the next thing I know Spencer calls me and says 'come on, I'm going down to P.J. Proby's hotel and we're going to write songs come on, come with me.'

'Ummm . . . okay.'

So we head down to Bondi to write songs with this guy. Spencer is really into it so I tag along. Why not?

The next thing we're in this little hotel room with a huge pile of tiny stubbies – stublets I call them, they're a small version of a stubby – piled up in the room. There's this MASSIVE, mountain-like pile of them in the corner of this hotel room. Tooheys New stublets. Of course we added to them. But it seemed almost like he was collecting them. Howard Hughes-style (no, I don't think they were filled with urine). They weren't stacked or anything. I could imagine him saying to housekeeping, 'Okay come in and do the room, fix the bed, change the towels – BUT DON'T TOUCH THOSE GODDAMN BOTTLES. LEAVE THE PILE OF BOTTLES RIGHT THERE.' Or perhaps he had just drank that much, just that day.

'Call me Jim,' he said as we drank together having exuberant conversations. He said he was friends with Dennis Hopper, and I have to say, that's who he reminded me of, mainly Hopper in *Apocalypse Now*, with a touch of Frank Booth from *Blue Velvet* lurking in the shadows.

Now, I've met some name-droppers in my time but P.J. takes the cupcake. Anybody, no, everybody you mentioned, and also people you had not mentioned, he knew. The Beatles? 'Yeah, John was an asshole.' 'Mick Jagger has a nine-inch penis', and 'This dirty $#!@%! turns up to one of my parties, so I kicked his arse down the stairs – I didn't know it was Jimi Hendrix'. After that I realised, 'Oh right, you're a complete dick.'

Randomly grabbing parts of mundane conversations was his favoured songwriting technique. At one point Spencer was talking to me about a Sunday afternoon residency I'd been doing at the Lansdowne Hotel on Broadway. I told him that I'd stopped and I wasn't sorry because it was ruining my Sundays. P.J. roars into life, 'GODDAMN IT THAT'S A HIT SONG – RUINING MY SUNDAYS.'

And then he'd go into a rant and try to rhyme some words with it. As far as I'm aware there's no royalty cheques out there with my and Spencer's names on them for 'Ruining My Sundays'.

Amazingly, this guy is still alive. But I can imagine Jimi Hendrix waiting on the other side waiting to kick his arse down the stairs.

SQUATTING IN SYDNEY

For me and a lot of the people I knew, there were three big things that made the late '80s a great time to be living in Sydney — being in a band, being on the dole, and being a squatter.

I wasn't always a squatter but it was a very important part of the underground cultural landscape of that time. There were a lot of empty houses and buildings back then and we felt a moral obligation to inhabit these places, not only to keep us housed but also to maintain them. Sometimes the actual owners of the building were happy to have squatters in there protecting the buildings from rats, pigeons and vandals.

But some people had the exact opposite moral position than we did. 'How dare you just move in to these places no one gives a shit about!'

The fact was there were empty buildings and houses every-where. Glebe had a whole street of houses people were squatting in. I knew people that were living in the Rank-Xerox building in Redfern. But nothing compared to The Gunnery. That was a complete scene all to itself.

The Gunnery was in Woolloomooloo, straight in front of the Finger Wharf and right near Harry's Café De Wheels. It's now part of the Art Gallery of New South Wales – a second site the gallery owns, rents out to people like Sydney Biennale, and occasion-ally puts on some exhibitions in. It was called The Gunnery because it was an old naval building used for storing ammunition.

Squats attracted very varied characters. True squatting is about the homeless getting a bit more organised in terms of finding and hanging on to accommodation. But all squats were different. There were political squats full of lefties and anarchists. There were punk squats. And of course there were squats occupied by folks with nowhere else to go.

At the Gunnery Squat in Woolloomooloo, 1990.

The Gunnery was an art squat. At first the deros of Kings Cross would crash there (literally) but slowly a central core of squatters started seeing the potential of the building for art and so began defining areas as being for this and that. It evolved to the point where you couldn't just flop there and live rent-free; to live in The Gunnery you had to be creative and contribute art.

By the time I moved in around 1988, The Gunnery had about 30 full-time residents – dancers, musicians, painters, and filmmakers. Picking up where the famous Yellow House of the '60s and '70s had left off, it had become this amazingly culturally diverse and creative space of cinema and theatre-like spaces.

My favourite was The Dome – a huge semi-circular room designed and used by the navy, we speculated, for target practice, in which a gunner would sit in this dome and simulate being in a war situation via projections. Whatever its original role The Gunnery repurposed it for performances.

The Gunnery represented the last breath of the squatter culture. Eventually the authorities formally seized back what they now recognised as prime waterfront real estate. One morning the police broke down the doors and dragged every-body out with cries of 'LET'S GET THESE SCUMBAGS THE FUCK OUT OF HERE!' Most people went quietly. They knew it was over. Despite what the police say, I still believe squatting was the right thing to do.

Which leads me to this little story . . .

In 1988 my girlfriend Andrea was living in a terraced house on Liverpool Street. These houses were tightly packed together and shared walls with the neighbours on either side. Andrea's neighbour was Marie, a kooky old lady with a cat. Marie was basically a shut-in so would only dash to the shops occasionally when it was absolutely necessary. Despite that (or because of it) she and Andrea got along nicely.

One night Marie's cat visited us, begging for food. We put it outside so it could return to its home, but it was persistent and immediately came back. That's when we noticed the smell. An alarming odour with a real tang that got stronger as we leaned towards Marie's back window. We suspected the worst, called the cops and sure enough when they broke Marie's door in, there she was upstairs in her bedroom at least two weeks dead. I won't go into detail but when a body is just left like that it becomes an incredible mess. Firstly it leaks bodily fluids from every orifice and eventually every pore and then . . . sorry.

What was left of Marie was taken away and we fed the cat for a while until it decided another neighbour's dwelling was more to its liking. Andrea's large dog Morris might've had something to do with that defection. Months went by and no one came to appraise or inhabit the house. Marie obviously owned the place so there was no landlord but surely she had family? If so, they never came and Marie's mail started to jam the letter hatch.

See where this is going?

Andrea and I had a friend named Tony Carmona. A truly lovely fellow, Tony had a wicked sense of humour and was one of gayest guys I ever knew.

One night we all decided it was time to take a good look inside Marie's place. We removed the louvres in the back porch window and climbed in, entering Marie's private world. She was a classic hoarder; stacks of newspapers were everywhere.

So much so, there was little room to move. Piles of rubbish and empty boxes took up every possible bit of space. There were framed paintings stacked in the corners in great numbers. Looking through them we realised Marie was the artist and that her body of work consisted of the same things painted over and over. There were 15 versions of kittens playing with a ball of string, 10 of the same bowl of fruit.

We decided we would clean the place up. This included sorting the junk and rubbish from the 'valuables' such as the paintings and furniture and whatever else we figured was personal to her. We stored all these things in one room and painted the entire interior of the house.

We did all this with the utmost degree of respect, often speaking to the spirit of Marie as we did it, talking her through the process and asking her permission as we went. During this process we came across nothing that indicated anyone had visited or been in contact with Marie for many years. Tony and I eventually moved in and we lived there happily together for a few months, always ready for the possible knock on the door. It came while I was away on tour. Tony was seen entering the front door by the police. Moral outrage ensued!

'WHAT IF IT WAS YOUR MOTHER?' the police said angrily. 'HOW WOULD YOU LIKE IT IF SOMEONE MOVED INTO YOUR DEAD MOTHER'S HOUSE?'

'I wouldn't let my mother die alone and forgotten,' he replied.

We were ejected and the house remained empty for many years afterward.

Lovely Tony Carmona died a few years later, another victim of the first decade of A.I.D.S. When Andrea became pregnant

I ended my squatting days and we moved into a flat in Bondi together. Our daughter Tuesday was born in October that year.

At no stage had I ever thought to myself, 'One day I'd like to have children and be a father.' I never got the chance to dream that dream because before I knew it, I was one. Witnessing the birth of my first child was a hurricane of mixed feelings. Joy and anticipation side by side with fear and anxiety. Andrea was so pure and strong through the pregnancy and labour. We went to a birthing centre in Paddington and they basically gave us a room and left us too it. With no drugs to help with the pain, Andrea delivered Tuesday with a totally natural birth. I think I was so in awe of her physical feat that it left me feeling inferior and almost unnecessary. Whatever physical challenges men put themselves through in the pursuit of 'being a man', we are just weak babies compared to what women go through during childbirth. There'd be a lot less people if men had to go through it.

And then there she was, this beautiful perfect little human. Tuesday.

We got the name from the actress Tuesday Weld and had chosen it long before she was born ... and then she was born on, you guessed it, a Tuesday.

Having kids at 25 might seem a logical time to start, but I was a rock'n'roller just starting to hit his stride. Late nights and sometimes many weeks away from home were not ideal conditions for parenting. When I was home in those early days of Tuesday's life, I did my best. But I was pretty useless.

Andrea was (and is) a great mother, but we were moving in different directions and so 18 months after Tuesday came into our lives, we ended it as a couple.

But we continued as parents and remain close to this day. Gradually I started to get the hang of this 'father' thing. It all seemed overwhelming at the time but now I'm glad. Having children at a young age means you're more likely to be still young enough to relate to each other as contemporaries when they grow up. Tuesday today is a remarkable human being. Another strong, intelligent, independent young woman. We share similar tastes in music. She's an animal-loving, school-teaching, Saints supporter and I couldn't be prouder.

Tuesday's arrival and fatherhood forced change on me and was a catalyst for a new life. For starters I left The Gunnery and went off the dole.

By now I was going overseas a bit with bands, touring regularly and playing gigs with someone, somewhere, most weekends. After doing that awhile it dawned on me that *I guess I have a career in music.*

I'd never thought of my working life in those terms. *Music* and *career* hadn't been words that ever went together in the same sentence for me before. It felt a bit weird thinking in those terms. But steadily it sank in.

MUSIC IS WHAT I DO.

THE CRUEL SEA

A lot of life is showing up.

Do that and the dividend can sometimes become *being in the right place at the right time.*

I mean if Mick and Keith hadn't met each other that day at the train station at Dartford, would the Rolling Stones have ever existed? They might have eventually found each other, but who knows?

For me, if . . . the Wadleys hadn't seen me going nuts at the Communist hall . . . and if Roger Grierson hadn't run into me at the bar at the New York Hotel and invited us down south . . . it could've been years till I left Brisbane . . . and so on and so on.

Or was it inevitable?

Things might have eventually happened, but would things have happened *this way*? I think about these things a lot because

I know now you can never really tell when you're at a cross-roads until you look back.

Back in 1987 I'd dropped around one Sunday afternoon to visit Peter Read at his Palmer Street flat. He said that he had to go somewhere and mix a band and that he'd see me later. I had nothing else to do so I said I'd go along too. He tried to discourage me from coming saying, 'You probably wouldn't like these guys.' But I persisted – I'm not sure why – and tagged along anyway even though I had no idea who the band was.

We caught a bus over to the Harold Park Hotel in Glebe and got there a few minutes before the band started.

Turns out the band was called The Cruel Sea.

I stood next to Peter at the mixing desk and noticed there was a lighting console no one was using so I started pressing switches and pushing faders. In that moment I became The Cruel Sea's lighting guy.

By the end of the first tune, I was in love. The band played guitar instrumental music. There were two guitar players, a bass player, a drummer and NO singer. They sounded like the Ventures, and indeed they played a few of their classic tunes. Occasionally they sounded like Booker T and the MGs. And occasionally they sounded like nobody else.

'What's this one?' I asked Peter.

'One of theirs,' he replied.

I loved this band and I loved them just the way they were. Honestly, I had no thought of wanting to join them or to collaborate with them at all, believe me. They wouldn't have had me anyway. I was still in Thug and although I loved them, I hadn't been involved in any conventional music for a long time.

Peter and I had a few beers with the boys after the show. They had a month-long residency at the Harold Park and I vowed to return and do their lights next week. The line-up then was Jim Elliot on drums, guitar player Dan Rumour, and the Corben Brothers, Dee and Ged, on bass and guitar. Ged and Dan were both on guitars and swapping lead, and they were incredible.

Ged was also playing in another band, The Lime Spiders, at the time. They were a '60s-style punk, garage-type outfit who were doing quite well and were a lot more commercially viable than any of the other bands around doing that '60s throwback thing. I have fond memories of Ged – a killer guitar player and another one of the easiest dudes you'll ever meet.

The Cruel Sea, 1989. From left to right: Danny Rumour, me, James Cruickshank, Jim Elliot (top) and Ken Gormley.

The idea of adding me as a singer came up inevitably during that time but I'd always say, 'I'm flattered but I want you to stay the way you are.'

There was probably 18 months where I resisted the urge to contribute in any way (apart from the lights). Then finally one night I was watching them at a house party and I *started hearing words*. Something changed that night. I started imagining the music differently and I now imagined a voice in there. Not necessarily MY voice, but Danny's guitar phrasing on this night now sounded like words to me. That's how we wrote 'Down Below'.

Dow dow doh
Down be low.

It wasn't so much my writing words for their sounds, it was more interpreting and dictating what I was hearing. I realised again just how good they were. And that if I didn't get on board someone else would.

So I reneged and ended up getting up with the band on their next gig, which happened to be at a party on a ferry in Sydney Harbour. Those one or two songs quickly became three or four songs and then more. Finally I found myself doing whole sets with them. They'd do three sets – one instrumental, one with vocals and then another one of instrumentals.

The band changed line-ups a few times over the next year and everyone was sad to see the Corbens go. But it finally settled on Jim, Dan, Ken Gormley and James Cruickshank. And me. Eventually we got to the point where we were writing songs together.

Then someone said, 'Let's make a record.'

DOWN BELOW

THE CRUEL SEA / 1989

A two-day session with Phil Punch, here we see the first
fruits of my collaboration with Danny Rumour and The
Cruel Sea. I've explained earlier how I wrote the lyrics to
some of these songs by literally interpreting the phrasing
of Danny's guitar playing. It's not bad, but the only songs
I still love are 'Dead Wood' and 'Margarita'. Jimmy Little
did a better version of 'Down Below' a few years later,
one that sounded less like an instrumental with words
attached and more like a real song. Despite being about
the marriage of my singing with Danny's music and the
growing chemistry between us, the best stuff on this
record is the instrumentals.

RECORD LABEL: *Red Eye*
CORE BAND MEMBERS: *Tex Perkins (vocals), Danny Rumour (guitar),
Jim Elliot (drums), Ken Gormley (bass).*

BLACK MILK

THE BEASTS OF BOURBON / 1990

Another mixed bag that took three days to record and
mix; this would be our last with Phil Punch. Being overly
ambitious we crammed WAY too many songs into this
session, leaving the album feeling rushed and unfocused.
And too much attention was given to the wrong songs.
It's got some good ones but these are not the best versions.
For instance, the version of 'Hope You Find Your Way
To Heaven' recorded in Vienna (and finally released on
From The Belly of the Beasts) shits all over the one found
here. But having said that, I must admit there were always
more songs from this album in our set list over the years
than from any other.

RECORD LABEL: *Red Eye*
CORE BAND MEMBERS: *Tex Perkins (vocals), Spencer P. Jones (guitar),
Kim Salmon (guitar), Boris Sujdovic (bass), James Baker (drums).*

YOU CALL THAT A QUESTION?

I have a reputation as an interview villain.

I've heard that people are intimidated about coming to interview me. Good. Be afraid, be very afraid.

I'm joking. For the most part I think I'm pretty affable and friendly – but *there have been moments* . . . and I'm guessing those moments have been talked about and word has spread to the point where these days some people think I'm going to bite their head off or upturn a table.

I suspect this all goes back to the first bunch of interviews I ever did for Polydor when The Beasts Of Bourbon released the *Black Milk* album in 1990.

It was one of those situations where they put you in an empty boardroom early in the day and 20 journos come through and they get 20 minutes each. Some of them you've

Me giving Tony Mott that look. Tony Mott using *that* lens.

known for a while and they know what they're talking about and you get on well and it's painless for all involved; interesting and fun even. Then there's the other ones.

A lot of journos ask, 'Do you mind if I tape this interview?' And I'm thinking, 'No, I'd rather you misquoted me, misunderstood me and misrepresented me.' But I usually say, 'Not at all, go ahead. I am.'

On this particular day I've been doing fine, I'm in a pretty good mood and everything's going well. I must say that towards the end of these sorts of days you can get a little more ratty. You've been talking about yourself all day and a lot of the time you've been saying the same things over and over.

So anyway, it's getting towards the end of the day and this woman comes in and she doesn't even say hello. Doesn't so much as look at me. She opens up her notebook and without looking up asks, 'What's the difference between this album and the last one?'

Something snapped in me, actually something broke; the facade I'd been holding up collapsed.

I just looked at her and said, 'Hey, let's not do this. You obviously don't have any interest or enthusiasm for this and to be perfectly honest I can't muster any enthusiasm for going through this with you, so let's just give it a miss shall we?' I didn't yell. I didn't throw anything. I just presented a logical alternative.

She was shocked. I mean, I wasn't angry, it was simply a case of 'come on, let's not bother'. Then, again without speaking she got up and went and found the PR person and explained how rude and difficult I was and then off she went. Did she ever write anything? I have no idea. This wasn't typical of my approach to interviews – but of course word got around.

The next one that caused a bit of trouble was a young journalist in Melbourne. Her first question was 'What's it like being Australia's Elvis Presley?' I couldn't believe what I was hearing.

'Really? Is that your question? For fuck's sake, I don't even understand how you arrive at the point where that becomes a question that you would entertain asking. Do you think that? Does anyone think that? For fuck's sake . . .'

Yes, I was flabbergasted. And then there were tears. Oh dear.

Since then, whenever she gets a chance she slags me off, more often than not to people who know me and tell me.

Fair enough. I hope it helps.

So the consequences of a bad interview can go on for years.

The result of these early interview encounters was that publicists would say to journalists before any interview was scheduled: 'You'd better know your stuff. If you don't really know your shit, he's going to tear you to pieces.'

Primed like this, the journalists were frequently terrified and expecting Lou Reed's demon offspring to walk in.

More often than not, if the journalist or broadcaster hasn't met me before, I sense that they're expecting me to be hard work so they're ready for a fight. Then they're surprised when they're unscathed at the end of it.

I'm not saying that I'm completely undeserving of my reputation but out of the thousands of interviews I've done there's very few that haven't gone well. Over the years I've honed different strategies to cope with the interview process. Doing them high, doing them straight, doing lots on the same day, doing just a few, doing them face-to-face, doing them over the phone. My favourite is just filling out a questionnaire.

It feels like writers see us as their adversaries, and we see them as ours. I accept them as part of what I do, but talking about myself can be excruciating. It's like helping someone do an autopsy on yourself.

So yes, I've been a prick, a jerk and an arsehole.

But I've also been interviewed by a lot of pricks, jerks and arseholes.

Look, to tell you the truth, I dread them. Any 'attitude' coming from me isn't arrogance, it's fear and defence.

KRISTYNA

Around the time I was earning my reputation as the worst interviewee for the Australian music press, The Beasts Of Bourbon toured Europe.

In Berlin for a gig, the press agency there needed someone to interview us. My reputation hadn't preceded me, so they sent an Australian girl living in Berlin at the time who was working for them. She was actually a photographer but they thought the mere fact she was Australian made her the best person for the interview.

So I'm sitting backstage at our Berlin show. In walked Kristyna.

She had moved from Brisbane to Berlin a few months prior. Kristyna had gone to East Berlin on a 'day visa' to visit a friend and buy some photographic equipment (these were the days of film and paper, etc). The press agency had convinced her to stay longer by saying the Wall was about to come down any day now and it would be great to be there when it happened. But 'any day now' turned into weeks and weeks. It was grim in the East and Kristyna had had enough.

As I was to learn, Kristyna is a can-do girl. And like me, she likes to *make things happen*. At this point her options were few. She could try to leave East Germany through a checkpoint and risk being prosecuted for overstaying her day visa. Or she could escape through NO MAN'S LAND.

Kristyna was staying in the East in an apartment that overlooked a cemetery near the wall. She noticed that people had started to chip away at the wall, making perfect foot holes up the face. Change was in the air. The Cold War was ending and the shoot-to-kill order had been revoked. So the choice was clear: *climb over the Berlin Wall*.

The plan was to play the lost tourist. So Kristyna took her camera, got a friend to give her a foot-up and started climbing up, then over, the wall.

Turns out there are really TWO walls – the East wall and the West wall. Kristyna is now in the barren 'death strip' between them. It's eerie – just her and lots of rabbits. She took a few snaps

Kristyna pretending to light a cigarette at a photo shoot.

then suddenly along came two angry guards rushing towards her yelling in German.

'What are you doing?!!'

'I'm just taking pictures,' said she.

They looked completely dumbfounded and confused. In English they said, 'Where did you come from?!'

'The West,' she replied.

So they marched her down the death zone and escorted her to the checkpoint and ejected her out into the West. Perfect!

The Berlin Wall would officially fall on 19 November 1989, a few months after Kristyna made her climb. This remarkable tale is typical of Kristyna, who's prepared to take risks if it becomes necessary. But only CALCULATED risks. She's not crazy, but man is she brave.

So, getting back to this gig. I'm backstage. This magnificent blonde girl walks through the door.

I immediately thought, 'Woah!'

I managed to stay fairly chilled around her because I remember thinking there was no way she'd be even remotely interested in me. That relaxed me and I didn't *try* to be charming (not that I wasn't).

In truth, Kristyna was unlike any girl that I had ever had anything to do with, yet she was very real and 'down to earth'.

Of course we were both from Brisbane so we talked a bit about that. Anyway, she did the interview and I didn't think all that much about it.

It wasn't until a few years later when I was playing in Brisbane that I saw Kristyna again. She went out with friends from work to see a band and I happened to be in that band. After the show we got talking and made the connection to Berlin. I was 26 and she was 21.

Kristyna was now doing some sort of production role at a commercial radio station, running and overseeing the place during the graveyard shift. Essentially her job was babysitting a radio station though the night. There was no one on air but somebody had to load up the CDs and so forth.

The next night I'm playing at The Orient in Brisbane. It's actually across from the building where Kristyna's radio station operates from.

The band room is above the pub so after the gig I climb out the window and stand on the awning to get a better look at the radio station. As fate would have it – this is really a true story – she sees me looking up and gets the idea that maybe I'm looking for her and that I'm interested, which is of course completely the situation.

Kids, this was old school. Back in those days you had to make an effort to contact people – you couldn't just text or email

them, send them a Facebook message or, God help me, look them up on Tinder! No, you had to stand on an awning on the top of a Brisbane hotel in the middle of the night and look at the building you think they're working in AND hope they're looking out the window at exactly the time you're looking up.

She was.

THIS IS NOT THE WAY HOME

The thing about The Cruel Sea was that on the right night, be it at a gig or in a specific moment in the studio, there could be, and often was, *magic*.

Metamorphosis.

In these moments we became greater than the sum of our parts. That's the place all bands try to get to. Out of the mystery of the music comes an alchemy created by the band but it's more than the band and it lifts you and makes everything flow. All we had to do was get on and ride that feeling.

We could also be fucking terrible. Sure there were no musical slouches in The Cruel Sea but there were times – lots of times – when it did not blend. On those occasions it felt like we were pushing shit up a hill with a teaspoon.

But the majority of the time it worked. And when The Cruel Sea clicked it was absolutely breathtaking and everything I ever wanted music to be. I'm not saying this as an objective observer of course, I'm just saying how it felt on the inside. And plenty of the time it was *totally exhilarating*.

From 1991 to 1995, The Cruel Sea received nothing but GLOWING reviews, especially live reviews. I mean, it got ridiculous. It got to the point where I didn't believe them. No one is THAT good. As musicians we'd all read overly positive live reviews to gigs we knew damn well were crap. But that didn't matter now. We had entered a critical vacuum; we could do no wrong. And that's a cancer for a band. Well it was for us.

Looking back it wasn't that we became conceited, more that we became cynical. Instead of enjoying the ride we asked, 'When's the backlash gonna come?' Cos believe me, we all knew in our bones it was gonna come.

In those days, we'd play anywhere we could and usually we'd go back three or four months later and there'd be a crowd twice as big.

Combined with all the work we did, Polydor did a good job as our record company. Our second album together, *This Is Not The Way Home*,was starting to take off, with songs all over the radio and videos screening on *Rage*. We had built the foundations of our fan base playing live, and the record company had built on that and sent record and show sales through the roof.

That made us very weary.

'We can't shove this down people's throats,' we'd tell them while trying to limit their use of television advertising and other promotional tools. It frustrated them no end. We'd worked very hard getting the band to this point, but having all come from the underground we were suspicious of success. Or a certain kind of success.

We wanted it but we wanted to shape it *our way* and not let it get more than we could handle. Of course it very quickly was more than we could handle. We wanted to sell records yes, but we didn't have that do-or-die ambition some of our contemporaries did who were happy to have success on any terms. We came along when we were just starting to peak as a band. We put out a record and the music industry actually *gave a shit*.

The Cruel Sea wouldn't have worked if it had happened two years earlier or two years later. We were the right band at the right time. We arrived in the post-Nirvana shake-up, smack in the middle of a whole bunch of changes in music, and we

Tony Cohen during The Three Legged Dog album mix. All notes and drawings are Tony's.

worked because we were playing good, true, honest music that people reacted to on a grassroots level. To have a hit record, a lot elements have to converge at the same time, and the stars aligned for us.

Some of that can be attributed to producer Tony Cohen.

Tony really pulled out all stops for The Cruel Sea. Tony had become even more of a ratbag since the early Beasts days. Now, he would be more and more crazed. He would mix louder and louder and with more and more reverb – everything was at full volume. Tony would mix it that way so the only way to listen to those records was at top volume. Play Tony's records of this era quietly and they seem a bit indistinct and washy but listen to them at full power and you get the full effect. *Awesome.*

Sometimes we used to try to trick Tony into doing a quick mix early because he'd always get very good initial sounds and recordings in the set-up. That was another thing that made Tony great to work with. He would get a good sound coming back at the band quickly and that would inspire everyone. Everyone would sit around listening to playbacks in the studio and go 'that sounds fucking GREAT', whereas some of the other producers and engineers we worked with would expect you just to put it down in the studio and say they'd make it sound better later, they'd fix it up further down the track. Tony was never like that. On a few albums Tony nailed it straightaway . . . *then* fucked it up down the track.

And as we went on we realised that the less Tony fiddled with a recording after he got it down initially, the better it was. We would sometimes use very rough, early mixes before all the later mad mixing went on. But having said that, as a good example of Tony's genius, *The Axeman's Jazz* is a live mix to tape but The Cruel Sea's *The Honeymoon Is Over* album is tweaked and fiddled to within an inch of its life and probably worth every twist of the knob.

The Cruel Sea, 1994. Older, cooler and grumpier.

THIS IS NOT THE WAY HOME

THE CRUEL SEA / 1991

Probably a five-day session with Tony Cohen. A record full
of good songs that don't sound their best. This was '91,
Tony's year of reverb. And I hadn't worked out how to sing
these songs as yet. Bad vocals and too much gated reverb
spoil this one for me. Despite these obstacles this won us
an ARIA award for best independent release (even though
it was through a major label) and sold enough to get us
our first Gold record. Yes, I'm sorry, I won't mention Gold
records and ARIA awards too much. I promise. (It didn't
happen that much).

RECORD LABEL: *Red Eye*
CORE BAND MEMBERS: *Tex Perkins (vocals), Danny Rumour (guitar),*
Jim Elliot (drums), Ken Gormley (bass), James Cruikshank (keyboards/guitar).

THE LOW ROAD

THE BEASTS OF BOURBON / 1991

This took a week of excess and debauchery with Tony Cohen at the controls. Luckily we had played and demoed most of these songs before this recording session, so we knew what we were doing. Again too much reverb and odd production elements spoil this for me (I'd love to remix this) but at least it was only 10 songs. After the ultra-eclectic *Black Milk*, this was to be our straight-ahead hard-rock album. I don't dig my performance on most of these songs – a bit too forced. There was a time during this period when I rightfully could've been accused of 'trying too hard'. Still, we had a tremendous amount of fun recording it. Tony mixed this so loud, few people could stand being in the room with him. (I think he preferred it that way.)

RECORD LABEL: *Red Eye*
CORE BAND MEMBERS: *Tex Perkins (vocals), Spencer P. Jones (guitar), Kim Salmon (guitar), Brian Hooper (bass), Tony Pola (drums).*

THE LOW ROAD

THE LOW ROAD

The Beasts Of Bourbon flew to the States and did a bunch of showcase shows, in June 1991, before *The Low Road* came out.

Lately I've found myself saying to people, 'I used to be in this horrible band called The Beasts Of Bourbon.' It's said for effect, I admit. But we *were* horrible. That was our stock and trade. We dealt in horrible. Although things would get much worse in a few years, the Beasts that went to the US in '91 were delightfully horrible. Our songs were no longer playful tributes to American blues; now they were calling cards for sleazebags.

Instead of Cajun Queens, it was Junky Girlfriends.

Boris and James had been too nice for this terrain. This was a job for Brian Hooper and Tony Pola. As soon as they joined the band everything changed. They brought an urgency to

Beasts, from left to right: Brian Hooper,
Spencer P. Jones, Tony Pola, Kim Salmon
and me.

all things in and around the band. The music was harder and
funkier and the revelry louder and wilder.

Tony was outrageous. He was thickset and animalistic but
strangely bookish at the same time. A magnificent, intelligent,
charismatic human being, but when he 'had that itch' he would
do *anything* to score. Things tend to disappear around funky
junkies, and Tony was no exception. Then *he* would disappear
for six months, sometimes at Her Majesty's pleasure.

Brian was wiry and good-looking and dressed like Ray
Liotta in *Goodfellas*. Brian was another one of these guys who
couldn't just have a bit, couldn't get just *a little* stoned. Like Tony,
Brian would think it a good idea to get hammered on smack

JUST BEFORE WE WENT ONSTAGE. Tony could handle it and I can't remember him ever playing badly. Ol' Brian on the other hand would be close to passing out onstage and playing like shit.

You *can* do it all: you can take drugs and play in a rock'n'roll band, but you just have to work out how to do it properly. It's all about the balance.

That's when the line is crossed with me – when you can't do your gig. That's it, I don't care who it is. If there's a gig, you have to be able to function enough to be able to do it – simple as that. After that you can do whatever the fuck you want to do.

As a drummer and a bass player, Tony and Brian played like gangsters. Brian had style and Tony was heavy and clever, with that John Bonham skill for being a hard hitter but with swing. Brian would've much rather been a guitar player than a bass player and he played like it. They'd known each other a long time and in a lot of ways were like brothers. They certainly fought like brothers. I'd never seen anyone push each other's buttons so skilfully. They would fight verbally pretty regularly, and occasionally it would lead to fisticuffs and stranglings.

But they loved each other like brothers as well, always ending up closer after the fight. 'I love you, you cunt.'

'Fuck you, you prick.'

And on it would go.

These days both of them are model citizens and clean as whistles, and have been for a decade. Back in 2003 Brian fell off a balcony and broke his back. Despite being told that he would never walk again, Brian determinedly rehabilitated himself to a point way past expectations. His recovery was a true Phoenix rising from the ashes episode, and was an inspiration to the rest of us Beasts. No one felt like they had the right to complain about their own discomfort after what Brian had been through. Brian's accident really showed what he was made of: *true grit.*

By the time the 1991 Beasts tour had finished, I needed time off.

My brother Robert hadn't been able to bear the fact that I'd got to America BEFORE HIM so at tour's end he insisted on meeting me in Los Angeles, with the plan being to buy a Cadillac and drive to New Orleans. I love Rob but I'll always be his annoying little brother and he'll always be my endearingly crazy big brother. This was gonna be HIS trip and he was gonna do the driving. Well, most of it anyway.

James Cruickshank was on that Beasts run of dates too as he'd played keyboards on two tracks on *The Low Road* so he tagged along with Robert and I.

We bought a 1973 Cadillac which I think is the largest car ever made. At 6 foot 4 I could lie fully stretched out on the back seat. We dubbed it The Shiny Beast, paid about a grand for it and set off for New Orleans. Driving south from LA is spectacular. When you get down to Arizona it starts to look like you're driving through a Road Runner cartoon, with all these strange monolithic rock formations.

We got as far as Yuma in Arizona before The Shiny Beast shat itself.

It was the transmission, and it needed AN ENTIRE NEW FUCKING TRANSMISSION. But shit, we were lucky we made it to civilisation and weren't stuck on the side of the road totally stranded in the desert with the coyote waiting for a delivery from the ACME company.

So we spent a couple of days in Yuma, drinking Budweiser by the pool. Nobody gets around without a car in Arizona, so we were questioned by police every time we went anywhere.

'What you boys doin'?'

'Just walkin' back to our motel officer.'

'Where you boys from?'

'Australia.'

'What the hell you boys doin' here?'

'Good question officer.'

As soon as we got the car back from the mechanics, James locked the keys in the boot of the car. Thankfully Yuma's best locksmith wasn't busy. And finally we were on our way again. We continued on south, driving through Texas, New Mexico and Louisiana, barely stopping along the way. Robert wanted to make up for lost time and was gonna drive hard all day and well into the night to get us to New Orleans as soon as possible.

We drove past the turn off to El Paso and I suggested stopping for something to eat and a quick look around. I mean, I'd always heard about these places in songs and movies.

'FUCK EL PASO,' said the king of the road.

When we finally got to New Orleans we looked for a hotel that was as close to the French Quarter as we could find. It had just rained so the streets had that beautiful wet sheen. We found a classic old place, not too far away from the action, with a bar and grill across the road where we drank beer, ate burgers and shot pool at all hours of the day.

We of course knocked over a few of the must-dos. Like seeing a band at the famous music club Tipitina's and eating a bowl of gumbo while listening to a crusty old dude singing in Creole with a zydeco band. A bartender we spoke to gave us the usual rundown: 'Whatever you do don't go to THAT part of town.'

So we immediately went to THAT part of town.

On that side of town were funky little homemade, probably unlicensed, bars, like Benny's, a gutted house with no walls, a dirt floor and band that wailed. Everywhere we went, we were constantly hassled and hustled by street drug dealers, which may or may not have had something to do with the way we looked. One actually tried to sell us lettuce wrapped in plastic saying it was pot. Did we look stupid too? Probably. This wasn't the Big Easy, this was the Big Hustle, and they weren't even very good at it. My favourite was this guy who suddenly appeared crab-walking alongside of me.

'I bet you twenty dollars I know where you got dem shoes you're wearing, man!'

I give him a quick look and then keep walking.

He jumps in front of me and says in a threatening tone.

'You got dem on your FEET motherfucker! Now gimme ma money!'

The big easy huh? Try harder dipshit.

After we're done with New Orleans, we have a conundrum:

what do we do with this fucking car? This magnificent vessel that has taken us across the greatest country on earth?

I know! What about if we drive over to Houston and give it to my old Thug buddy Lachlan McLeod who's living there at the moment? It was only about five or six hours drive so the plan was that we'd do that, give the car to him, then fly to LA and catch a plane home to Australia.

A plan. A good plan.

We arrived in Houston pretty late at night and the flight the next morning was fairly early, which made sleep an inconvenience. So we asked Lachlan and his girlfriend Stacey Rae if they thought they could help get us something to keep us up until the flight at around 7 am the next morning.

Looking for trouble.

They suggested we could get some crack from the gangs down at the super-market car park as they are ALWAYS there. I was only thinkin' coffee but hey . . . So we think about this for three seconds and decide hmmm . . . okay, we'll do that. Let's give it a shot. We're leaving for LA the next morning so it's not like we're going to get hooked on crack in the next six hours, is it? Plus it felt like the tourist thing to do.

Things to do and see in America.

See the Statue of Liberty.

Visit the Grand Canyon.

Score some crack. I've heard it's all the rage over here. Quite moreish apparently.

Next thing you know we're driving down to a desolate shopping centre. We turn into the car park and just wait – FOR SECONDS and then BANG – NWA are all over the car. And they're not just around the car – they're in the car, heads in all the windows saying, 'How you doing man?' and we're all 'Very well thank you' while Stacey Rae is doing the deal. When the deal is done it's a quick thank you and off we drive into the night.

Lachlan opens up the purchase when we're out of range and sighs, 'Oh shit, It's just SOAP. They've sold us soap.' Damn!

Stacey Rae is not happy. She says in this classic Texas twang, 'I'm not letting that happen in ma hometown. That's just OUTRAGEOUS. It's downright rude. I'M GOING BACK TO TEACH THOSE BOYS A LESSON.'

Wait just a minute there, Missy!

We try to explain that it's fine. Shit happens. Let's just leave it. 'Really, Stacey Rae don't worry about it.'

But she's driving. She's already turned the car around and before I can physically restrain her we're back at the car park and she's out of the car and heading in the direction of the dealers and waving her finger at them with this 'How dare you' attitude.

Me? I'm waiting for us to get shot.

TEX

I say to Robert, 'GET IN THE DRIVER'S SEAT. DRIVE OVER THERE. LET'S GET HER AND GET THE FUCK OUT OF HERE.'

By the time we get to Stacey Rae it's all looking very, very heavy. Stacey Rae is making a forceful consumer complaint to a crack-dealing gang leader and his minions are swarming all over the car, heads in the windows saying, 'Give us a beer man', so yes sure, we give them some beers.

Suddenly it all turns very nasty. Cruickers gets a beer bottle broken over his head. I'm in the back seat, suddenly a knife appears through the window and comes up tight under my chin. Instinctively – with a knife against my precious vocal chords – I manage to pull out my wallet and hold it up. Instantly the whole situation ends and they vanish with the new eel-skin wallet I'd just bought at the markets in New Orleans.

So we leave with no drugs and no money and no wallet. I was fuming. 'How are you still alive?' I angrily inquire of Stacey. 'That was the stupidest thing I've ever seen! If you think that kind of thing's a good idea, why the fuck hasn't someone ended you by now?'

Next thing I know we arrive at some dude's house. They're having a small party – there's music, booze and lots of sweet cousin cocaine. Why the fuck didn't we just come straight here? We end up telling the story of our night to the nice folks there and the guy whose party it is takes it all in then beckons us into his room and opens up a drawer full of handguns.

See, he and his mates are all fired up about this experience we've had and now they're talking about a plan of going back there in a different car and then when the guys in the gang come over going BANG, BANG, BANG and shooting them all in the kneecaps and then driving away.

I'm thinking, *Well, this is what happens in America.*

There was actually a minute when it SOUNDED LIKE A GOOD IDEA.

I never did try crack but I certainly got a taste of the whole American saga of drugs, gangs and guns. This guy with the handguns was really prepared to facilitate us getting revenge for a drug deal gone bad. It made me realise that if you don't have a minute to pause and reflect then *shit can happen*. And very quickly. It's what can – and does – happen all over America every hour of every day.

DOG BLESS AMERICA.

FROM THE BELLY OF THE BEASTS

THE BEASTS OF BOURBON / 1993

Half live album and half outtakes and rarities, this has some great stuff and some real pieces of shit as well. Interesting live recordings from the mid-'80s document the fact that Stu Spasm, Brad Shepherd and Graham Hood were briefly in the band. There are better AND worse versions of various songs from the first 10 years of the band. But a few gems are hidden in the rubbish tip of an album that this is.

RECORD LABEL: *Red Eye*
CORE BAND MEMBERS: *Tex Perkins (vocals), Spencer P. Jones (guitar), Kim Salmon (guitar), Brian Hooper (bass), Tony Pola (drums), Brad Shepherd (guitar), James Baker (drums), Stu Spasm (bass).*

IGGY

I love Iggy Pop.

For me, the first three Stooges albums are like masterclasses in primal rock'n'roll.

All three are distinctly different from each other, and all three are absolutely vital. The Stones have more great songs but Iggy is where I live. Deep down, everything I do has a little Iggy in it.

I first met Iggy Pop at the 1993 Big Day Out. That second Big Day Out just had a really special feeling about it. In later years there remained a great vibe among all the Australian groups on the tour, but '93 was the only time I observed Australian and international groups hanging together and having fun. Nobody was acting like 'rock stars' and the cool people dropped their guard a bit – even Nick Cave. I mean, on one of the days between shows I went to Magic Mountain in

Adelaide with Kim Gordon and Lee Ranaldo from Sonic Youth, the boys from Mudhoney and Michael Franti from Spearhead. All of us riding the waterslides down at Glenelg for the afternoon and laughing like kids. It was great.

But Iggy was special.

The Beasts Of Bourbon were doing the Big Day Out side-shows with him that year so we saw quite a bit of him and his band. It was a particularly good time to see him as he had a great band and played a lot of early stuff, mostly Stooges. He had an odd habit at the time, of doing half the show with his pants around his ankles. It was strange as it restricted his movement, waddling about when he wanted to move, big dick and saggy arse swinging.

My favourite memory of that tour was driving back to Sydney after the show in Canberra and stopping at one of those servos on the highway. As we rummage through the fridges and shelves for pies, chocolate bars and cigarettes in walks Iggy, who joins us in our hunt for quality late night on-the-road snacks. We discuss our various tastes and tolerances. THE ART OF EATING SHIT ON THE ROAD.

A few months later The Cruel Sea were in America playing, of all things, an afternoon spot at CBGB. It was a showcase – a record company and media gig – but still a show, even if the idea of playing CBGB on an afternoon still sounds a little strange.

Our sound check had resulted in the PA system ceasing to function. Seriously, by the time we were meant to go on stage there were no monitors and no vocal PA. Faaarrrck.

Then, just before we were meant to go onstage, someone from the venue comes back and asks if I can come to the front door. They need me to come and see if I know 'a dude' who's turned up and asked to get in even though they're not on the guest list. So I go out the front and there at the door looking meek and mild with hopeful puppy dog eyes is IGGY POP and his wife.

IGGY FUCKING POP. Just let that sink in.

I'm still staggered that Iggy could come to a place like CBGB and no one working there recognises him, let alone that they're actually questioning whether they should let IGGY POP in or not?! This is CB fucking GB's! Wasn't Iggy backstage every night getting blow jobs during the '70s? Or giving blow jobs? I can never remember which.

Either way there should be a fucking shrine to him somewhere in this dump.

That night at CBGB in New York, 1993.

Iggy explained to me that he'd read about the show in *The Village Voice*. It would have just said something like, '4 pm – From Australia, The Cruel Sea'.

I can't remember even telling him I was in another band called The Cruel Sea, as I was in the Beasts when we met.

So to the door 'person' I explain that *YES, it is okay to let Iggy Pop into the CBGB gig.*

Maybe I shouldn't have. It was fucking terrible. The PA never got working so I had to go around physically from table to table and sing to people who were within earshot.

I never go down without a fight.

NEW YORK

A few months later in New York, our manager, Wendy Boyce-Hunter, was talking to record companies and even though I didn't really need to be there, Kristyna and I had tagged along.

Wendy was in contact with Sonic Youth's management, Gold Mountain – and before I knew it Kim Gordon and Thurston Moore had invited us around to their apartment.

We hung out for a while until they said they were going to a *Saturday Night Live* filming where Nirvana was performing and did we want to come along? I wasn't going to say no. This was *Saturday Night Live* in late 1993 – the height of the show.

So we cruise down to NBC studios where our names are on the guest list and head upstairs and go backstage. There are the Red Hot Chili Peppers, J Mascis from Dinosaur Jr. and what seems like everyone else in the top echelon of the cool rock'n'roll scene at the time just hanging in the hallway. That's what made it even more awkward, people weren't in some green room drinking beer and eating barbecue Shapes, they were all just milling about in the hallway. But I guess this was Nirvana on *Saturday Night Live* at the height of their fame. If you're a person that likes to be seen to be where *it's* happening *this* was where it was happening.

We follow Kim and Thurston into a dressing room and there's Nirvana, all sitting around looking nervous. Courtney Love is there too, of course, fussing like a mother hen – 'You're not wearing that on TV, Kurt.'

Outside the stars are filing by. Charles Barclay and RuPaul, Dana Carvey and Mike Myers, Adam Sandler and Chris Rock.

For fuck's sake . . .

I felt extremely uncomfortable. I realised that I was out of my league, that I wasn't one of these people. *I really don't belong here* . . . Nice as it was for these people to invite us along, it was all too much. Sonic Youth may be able to cruise through these situations but I shouldn't be here. If I was Nirvana I wouldn't want me here.

Nirvana played and the whole show finished and Kim and Thurston invited us on to another party. But I had to get out of there. These were the most famous rock people on the planet at that time and there I was with them. I'd been invited and accepted by these ultra cool A-listers but I'd never felt like more of a jerkoff B-grader in my life.

So instead of partying with the kings and queens of grunge, instead of rollin' with rock'n'roll royalty, Kristyna and I excused ourselves, muttered something about jet lag, caught a cab back to the hotel and watched a *Twilight Zone* marathon on TV.

Looking back this was probably interpreted as rudeness or arrogance, but I was quietly freaking out. They say you should never meet your heroes. I've met people whose music I've loved for years and when they turned out to be dicks I couldn't listen to another note. The top of the mountain is weird and uncomfortable for me. There's just too much pressure up there. You're too exposed. Everyone's watching. Your inner dialogue says DON'T FUCK UP. I realise that sounds paranoid, but it's true. I was already feeling the downside of success and had done pretty much as soon as it arrived with The Cruel Sea. That night in New York at *Saturday Night Live* I felt like I'd walked into a living rock magazine and it just felt way too weird.

I was the wrong guy at the right time.

Maybe Kurt felt it too. Six months later he was gone.

THE HONEYMOON IS OVER

THE CRUEL SEA / 1993

I think this took, I dunno, let's say three weeks to record, maybe a little more. Tony really squeezed this one, tweaking and fiddling for days at a time on one song. (I can't stand the gated reverb on the snare drum.)

It was designed to sound good and get played on the radio and that's exactly what happened. Five ARIA awards and a quarter of a million sales, this thing was very popular. But unfortunately the title was particularly prophetic. The honeymoon WAS over – not with the public or the critics; we had fallen out of love with ourselves and each other.

RECORD LABEL: *Red Eye*
CORE BAND MEMBERS: *Tex Perkins (vocals), Danny Rumour (guitar), Jim Elliot (drums), Ken Gormley (bass), James Cruikshank (keyboards/guitar).*

THE HONEYMOON IS OVER

Nirvana's arrival had marked the end of the old guard.

All those established '80s bands had had their time and the music industry was noticing the old stuff wasn't selling as well anymore and there was all this other fresh meat around.

The Cruel Sea were fortunate to have come along just before this revolution happened, and when it did grunge was what the record companies were trying to sell. The Cruel Sea were very definitely not grunge but we fitted in at a time when an independent band playing good music could actually pull crowds *and* sell records.

So in those early '90s everything was coming together for The Cruel Sea. We'd been touring everywhere and steadily building up crowds. The line-up was settled and the band was playing great, with all the trappings of a group on the move – a manager, a record company, great album and show reviews and a fast-growing fan base.

With everything solidifying I'd started to see the potential of the band to do the mainstream thing. There were a few records around at the time – Lenny Kravitz's *Mama Said* and Diesel's *Hepfidelity* – that weren't so much an influence on our music, but that had got me thinking that if records like that can get played on the radio then why the hell can't the music of The Cruel Sea?

On a grassroots level every time we went out and played I could see the momentum picking up and the band getting bigger. I never really got thinking about whether I actually wanted real success. Or what success actually might mean to me. When you make music you naturally want people to hear it, and to my way of thinking at the time, the more the better.

But believe me, somewhere in that process there's a line you cross. And when you cross that line and it goes to that next level, boy, you better be ready for it.

By the time we got around to recording *The Honeymoon Is Over*, we all kinda had the attitude that this album was gonna do the business. We as a band, along with Tony Cohen, were trying to get people to embrace what we were doing, rather than saying, 'This is our sound, take it or leave it.' We were making appealing music that we liked. So why shouldn't others?

By now I'd worked with many different people and used many different writing techniques. But the most tried and true for me had proved to be *adding words to existing music* as I had from the outset with Cruel Sea instrumentals inspiring the sound of the words. Working that way, I heard the music with fresh ears and it spoke to me on an instant and emotional level.

Where does this music take me?

What does this music want me to say?

How can I serve the song?

That's the bottom line for me. Because I'm not someone with a burning need to SAY SOMETHING. I honestly don't know what is going to be said when I start writing a song. I simply get a sniff and then chase that rabbit wherever it goes. For me, that's the fun of it.

Writing songs can also be like writing jokes. I love a good punchline or one-liner.

The song 'The Honeymoon is Over' is all based around the lines:

> *Gonna send you back to wherever the*
> *hell it was you came*
> *Then I'm gonna get this tattoo changed*
> *to another girl's name*

Before we went into the studio to record, I had met a bloke that had gone through this very dilemma. *What to do with the old girlfriend's name written on you after she's not your girlfriend anymore and you now have a new girlfriend who wants HER name there instead?*

I thought that scenario was pretty funny and so that was the beginning of that song. Before the music, even before the name of the song, that line was enough to give me a sniff.

TEX, DON + CHARLIE: YEARS OF THE ROOSTER

The first time I saw Charlie Owen play guitar was the night we met in Stockholm in 1991.

The Beasts Of Bourbon were playing a double bill with Rob Younger's band The New Christs and Charlie was his current axe man.

I stood in the audience and watched this guy play incredibly soulful rock'n'roll guitar. It seemed like he was playing lead and rhythm guitar at the same time. I was impressed.

But I was foolish enough to walk back into the Beasts' band room and say to my guitar-playing band mates, 'I think he might be the best guitar player I've ever seen!'

I said this out of enthusiasm, not thinking of how my statement would go down and who I was saying it to.

'Oh really?!' said Kim Salmon.

'You're just stoned!' said Spencer P. Jones.

It's true, I was, but let me tell you, he was good.

When I spoke to Charlie later that night, he was full of homesick tour-weary whingeing. 'I'm so sick of rock'n'roll,' he said. 'I just want to go home.' Fair enough, I know the feeling. They were nearing the end of their run and we were just starting. Eight weeks in a van can wear you down.

About a year later back in Australia I was asked to do some acoustic sessions on ABC radio. There was a lot of it about at the time, the whole 'unplugged' thing was hot. They wanted me to team up with Don Walker, songwriter and keyboardist of the very famous band Cold Chisel.

I didn't know a lot about Don's post-Chisel work, but I had heard he'd recently been working with none other than Charlie Owen. 'Okay,' I said. 'But get him to bring that Charlie Owen fella.'

We met and rehearsed at Don's place in Kings Cross. Don was a tall good-looking gentleman with a country undertaker's vibe. He was slow talking, and possessed an Australian accent with so much drawl no one could ever doubt where he came from. Don would always be smoking a cigar. These were the days where you could smoke just about anywhere and you'd always know where Don had been – you could smell him a mile away.

The radio session went really well. So well that straightaway it seemed obvious we should do more. By now Charlie was playing dobro slide guitar as well as electric and acoustic. I had a few new songs that weren't quite right for the Beasts or The Cruel Sea and of course Don had a bag full of his own so we decided to record an album.

Tony Cohen was the obvious man for the job of recording us and we asked Shane Walsh to play double bass and Jim White of the Dirty Three to play drums. The last, but very tasty, ingredient was Garrett Costigan on mournful, but beautiful, pedal steel.

The music we made was a blend of folk blues and country, I guess. But not Tamworth or Nashville country – this had an urban feel. The songs felt like they came from the back alleys of Kings Cross and the characters in them walked straight out of a TAB and into a strip club. It was grubby and world weary, but with the occasional moment of purity of heart.

Don sang a few of his songs, I sang a few of his songs and also a few of mine. It turned into a good balance. More than once people have compared the dynamic as similar to Kris Kristofferson and Willie Nelson singing together. But it's not just our voices; Charlie's 'voice' is his guitar playing which is just as lyrical as our vocals.

Tex, Don & Charlie's *Sad But True* is one of my favourite albums that I've been involved with. Everyone enjoyed making it, and it received a warm reception from the public and critics alike. So it's hard for me to explain why it took 12 years for us to make a second album. I guess time slips away from you when you're not careful. Admittedly, we all had plenty of other things to do. But still, 12 years? *Come on.*

When we finally did come together to record the *All Is Forgiven* album in 2005, we were fortunate to be able to assemble the same band. Despite Jim White living overseas, he was in town just long enough to contribute his unique drumming to the album. Of course we had to have Shane back – he wasn't a fancy player but his understated style was an important part of the sound we again were after.

All Is Forgiven is also one of my favourites. It felt good for me to be playing with these guys again and I'm sure we promised ourselves it wouldn't take us so long to record another one.

Then in 2010 Shane died of a heroin overdose. It was a sad and tragic demise for a much-loved rascal of a man.

Charlie, Don and I played in the Grey Street chapel where Shane's funeral was held, but after that farewell the thought of playing without Shane seemed too painful to even consider for a while so the next album would have to wait. How long? How about 12 years?

That's right – Tex, Don & Charlie have recorded an album again, and again with a gap of exactly 12 years between it and the last one. Not that we meant to, and not that it really means anything, but I realised we have only released albums in the Chinese years of the rooster. That's weird huh? No?

Anyway, this time we asked Steve Hadley to play bass and Charley Drayton played drums. *STAND BY FOR MASSIVE NAME DROPS.* Steve's played with everyone from Stevie

Wonder to Archie Roach and Charley's played with everyone else (including Keith Richards).

BOOOOM BOOM BOOOOM.

And of course once again Garrett plays pedal steel like no one else. These guys were perfect as our musical accomplices.

The album is called *You Don't Know Lonely* and I think it's another beauty, worthy to sit alongside the other two. See you in 12 years, fellas.

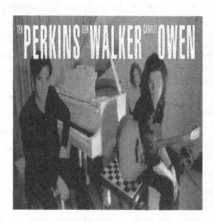

SAD BUT TRUE

TEX, DON & CHARLIE / 1993

A three-day session with Tony again, recorded at
Metropolis studios in Melbourne. One of my favourite
records, everyone brought the goods for this one. Charlie,
Don, Shane Walsh, Garrett Costigan and Jim White – I
think I'm the weakest link here. I still hadn't learned how
to sing at this point; still, it's a great collection of songs
and Charlie's dobro is the key element. Tony really knew
how to record Charlie's guitars and although people said he
wasn't a singer I think Don's vocals are more interesting
and authentic than mine and stand the test of time.

RECORD LABEL: *Red Eye*
CORE BAND MEMBERS: *Tex Perkins (vocals/guitar), Charlie Owen (guitar/dobro),
Don Walker (vocals/piano/organ), Jim White (drums), Shane Walsh (double bass),
Garrett Costigan (pedal steel), Warren Ellis (violin), Kim Salmon (Jew's harp).*

MONDAY MORNING COMING DOWN . . .

TEX, DON & CHARLIE / 1995

Originally recorded live as a bonus disc for a second run of
promotion for *Sad But True*, we realised that would mean a
whole lot of people who bought *Sad But True* when it first
came out would have to buy the album again to get *Monday
Morning Coming Down*. So we insisted that it be released
as an album unto itself. So basically it's a collision of record
company logic and artist morality. It probably shouldn't
exist at all, being comprised of most of the previous album
and a few wobbly covers.

RECORD LABEL: *Red Eye*
CORE BAND MEMBERS: *Tex Perkins (vocals/guitar), Charlie Owen (guitar/dobro),
Don Walker (vocals/piano/organ), Jim White (drums), Shane Walsh (double bass),
Garrett Costigan (pedal steel), Kim Salmon (Jew's harp).*

ALL IS FORGIVEN

TEX, DON & CHARLIE / 2005

This took about 10 days with our old mate Phil Punch who
I hadn't worked with for 15 years. Same band as the first
TDC record, 12 years later. Another that resides in my
top self-rated albums. 'Whenever It Snows' is one of the
few well-written songs I've ever been involved with. Don
successfully brought the humour and the sleaze with his
killers, 'Another Night In' and 'Harry Was A Bad Bugger'.

RECORD LABEL: *Red Eye*
CORE BAND MEMBERS: *Tex Perkins (vocals/guitar), Charlie Owen (guitar/dobro),
Don Walker (vocals/piano/organ), Jim White (drums), Shane Walsh (double bass),
Garrett Costigan (pedal steel), Kim Salmon (Jew's harp).*

YOU DON'T KNOW LONELY

TEX, DON & CHARLIE / 2017

As usual, 12 years after the last one, we released the third TDC album. We're like the Halley's Comet of the music biz. It was hard moving on after Shane's death but we finally decided to go ahead and begin work on a new album in early 2016. This time Steve Hadley played double bass and Charley Drayton played drums. These guys nailed their contributions and I really believe we have an album worthy to stand alongside the other two. This time I thought it was my responsibility to bring the sleaze, so I did, with what I think is the best song I've written for a while: 'A Man In Conflict With Nature.' I think I sing all right on this album, but Don's singing has matured a lot since we started 24 years ago. Charlie brings his class to all the songs he graces and Garrett once again splashes the ethereal treacle of his pedal steel wherever we need some mystery and emotion.

RECORD LABEL: *EMI*
CORE BAND MEMBERS: *Tex Perkins (vocals/guitar), Charlie Owen (guitar/dobro), Don Walker (vocals/piano/organ), Jim White (drums), Shane Walsh (double bass), Garrett Costigan (pedal steel), Kim Salmon (Jew's harp).*

FOOTY

In 1993 I saw the famous photo of Nicky Winmar, the one where he pulls his St Kilda jumper up after a game against Collingwood and points to the skin of his torso.

It was a spur-of-the-moment gesture to the Collingwood supporters who were racially abusing him at the time, as if to say, 'I'm black and I'm proud.' That photo was all over the major Melbourne newspapers that weekend and soon was being talked about everywhere.

That photo drew me in like a magnet. I realised that yes, the photo was all about racism, but for me it was more personal. It was one man against a mob – an ugly hateful spitting mob. Nicky was standing defiantly, not in anger but in pride.

Gandhi couldn't have done it better.

Digging deeper, I learned how Australian Rules had

originated from a game played by Australian aborigines. Marngrook involved the kicking and catching of a wombat skin stuffed with grass and it had been played for thousands of years by the blackfellas.

This game was older than the pyramids. That blew my mind.

Apart from maybe music and art, it's possibly the oldest cultural activity still going. If the blackfellas have been here 40,000 years have they played marngrook for 40,000 years?

Quite possibly. I mean, why wouldn't they?

I had never considered that primitive cultures had a need for sport. It awakened a fascination in me and I quickly arrived at the idea that there is something sacred and mystical, but also political about this game. That this is truly OUR game, not something brought here by the Poms but born of this land, and no other. Not even the Kiwis get it. *It's ours.*

I had developed a bit of an interest in the Swans when I was living in Sydney.

Dale Lewis was my favourite at the time, mainly because he always had shit all over his face. In an era of guys with neat hair who looked professional – people like Wayne Carey – Dale Lewis was the complete opposite with his fallen-down socks and filthy straggly hair. I was automatically attracted to him because he looked so different to everyone else.

Another that caught my eye was Darryl White of the Brisbane Bears. With his lanky lackadaisical demeanour Darryl was all arms and legs as he recklessly launched himself at every contest. Now here was a guy I could relate to!

But even though I had jumped on the bandwagon of the

Swans when Tony 'Plugger' Lockett was playing for them, I was never what you could call a Sydney supporter. I came from Brisbane so maybe I should have been looking at the Bears.

After my marngrook epiphany, I started watching Aussie Rules games when I was around people from Melbourne. They had a much different attitude to footy than people from Sydney and Brisbane. People in Melbourne might go to the art gallery and then to the MCG and watch the footy, then go to a nightclub or see a rock band that night. They'll do that all in the same day and see no conflict or strangeness about that – which there isn't. They're all art forms that express different parts of the human psyche.

I wasn't yet a committed follower but just as I had felt my way into the rock'n'roll world, I was looking at football and trying to find out where I belonged. Everything became clear when I moved to Melbourne in 1995 and lived in St Kilda. It all just seemed to fit into place that St Kilda be my team. This is my turf and this is my team.

The 2010 AFL Grand Final – or should I say grand finals – were something else of course, especially as a St Kilda supporter. I had very mixed emotions watching those games, especially the first game, which ended in a draw.

I remember that with a few minutes to go we were up by five points and we were playing well and had the momentum. And I had this moment where I realised that we were possibly going to win the Grand Final – the first time St Kilda had done that since 1966. We had won just one premiership in 150 years and once again it was against Collingwood.

Obviously I was thrilled about this – but what was interesting was that I had this other thought, that after we won, everything was going to change. The whole culture of St Kilda and the club and its supporters would never be the same again.

I'd initially got onboard with St Kilda partly because of where I was living in Melbourne, but also because of its history of NOT winning. That was a big thing for me. I find a culture based on struggle much more attractive than the culture of a club that's on top of the ladder and won the most premierships. A lot of people are born into their allegiance to a club but a lot of people would pick Essendon or Collingwood – Carlton or Hawthorn – just because they have a history of being successful and being big teams and doing well.

For me the attraction to St Kilda was the opposite of all that. It was the history of St Kilda and the fact that it was based on difficulty and always being the underdogs. I was attracted to the fact that they'd never won another Grand Final because I thought when it did happen it would be that much sweeter. Being a St Kilda supporter is both character building and soul destroying at the same time.

And here we are, about to win a second premiership and I had a moment when I was realising that all that culture is going to be wiped clean if we win. Everything is going to be different. We, as St Kilda – the club and the supporters – won't be the same people anymore. We won't be who we are at this moment. I knew that everyone in and behind the club wanted this win desperately but at the same time I had this strong sense that all the things that we built our characters on would be gone. All that culture of adversity and struggle was going to be wiped clean. We'd be just another team that has won a couple of premierships.

I'm a Catholic. I look for suffering. It's what defines me. I'm joking, but seriously, it's all about the struggle. If things come too easily I don't respect them. I think about my friend Bob Murphy, captain of the Western Bulldogs AFL team, in that context and what he's gone through, and of course his experience is arguably much worse than mine. His team won, but he couldn't play. That must be the strangest mix of emotions. A collision of joy and regret. But I'm sure he's not insane enough to have had those sorts of thoughts with the Western Bulldogs.

That moment I had at the Grand Final was very much like one of those cinematic moments when all the sound dies down and there's just the inner dialogue: 'Are we going to win? . . . Shit . . . We're going to win . . . What happens then? . . .' Outside my immediate vision was all blurry and I was pondering these issues while watching the game being played right in front of me. Then Collingwood got a goal and then it was, BACK TO REALITY. Phew.

I realise even thinking this stuff is seriously fucked up on one level. The very notion that I didn't want St Kilda – my team –

to win is insane. But there was this part of me that was seriously worried that we were about to lose our culture.

The Saints are one point down with less than two minutes to go, Lenny Hayes kicks the ball 60 metres deep into the forward pocket. A true 'last ditch effort', the kind of physical feat that's usually followed by triumph. It was heroic, it was epic . . . it, didn't bounce well for Milney. Through for a point. Draw.

And of course I was back for the replay. That was soul destroying. Except that it kept my theory intact. Even though I had those thoughts, the actual game was excruciating. I try not to even think about it. They got four unanswered goals in the first quarter and they were on a bit of a roll, and then Nick Riewoldt had the ball kicked to him alone in the goal square and no-one seemed to be around. He casually turned towards the goal and jogged in to kick what should have been a certain goal. Heath Shaw came out of fucking nowhere. He must have been 20 metres away and suddenly he's THERE and Riewoldt is on the ground.

We were gone in that moment. It showed how up the Pies were, and how . . . whatever the fuck we were.

And that's the last thing I'll say about footy. I promise.

ARIA NIGHTMARE

My most famous public meltdown was at the ARIA Awards in 1994.

Well, not so much a meltdown as a volcanic eruption.

The Cruel Sea had just won a whole lot of awards for *The Honeymoon Is Over* – five of them in fact. We'd won Single Of The Year, Album Of The Year and Best Album, Best Group and Song Of The Year, so everyone was pretty buoyant and ready to party.

In those days they'd give you your award on the night so afterwards you're walking around high as a satellite holding all these large pointy hunks of metal. I changed all that.

So we arrive at an afterparty, thrown by rooArt Records at a warehouse in Ultimo and I'm holding two of these awards. Someone offers me a drink. Not having a free hand I spin and drive the ARIA award into the wall behind me, turn back and gratefully accept the drink. The ARIA award stays in the wall as I begin talking to Kev Carmody, the Aboriginal Buddha figure. Things are momentarily calm.

Then I look across the room and there's some guy wrestling with Kristyna. He has handfuls of her long blonde hair and is trying to drag her to the ground. She later tells me that she'd been watching him staggering around the room physically molesting women. He was a menace.

At the time I didn't know any of this. I just snapped. I launched myself across the room and started belting into him with whatever I had in my hand – which just happened to be a stubby and luckily not a very, very pointy and potentially lethal ARIA. This was not something that I put though any kind of thought process, this was *pure animal instinct*.

Suddenly it's chaos – like the disco shoot-out scene in *Scarface*. People are screaming, bodies and bouncers flying everywhere, blood is spurting and folks are scattering, all with a disco soundtrack and moving coloured lights from a mirror ball. In the middle of this melee there's a pile of writhing bodies and I'm at the bottom of it.

I struggle free of the pack, crawl to my feet and continue my rampage. I was INSANE. In that moment I wanted that motherfucker dead.

At one stage I remember a familiar face in front of me screaming:

'TEX! TEX! STOP! STOP!'

'GRRRRRR!'

Through the red mist I register that the face is Molly Meldrum's. Not a face that ever calmed me down.

I push Molly out of the way leaving a huge bloody hand-print on his nice white shirt.

'GRRRRRRRRRRRRR!'

There's broken glass and blood everywhere, mostly mine. This prick has a hard head but it doesn't stop me raining punch after punch down upon it.

Finally I'm dragged away. It's time to leave.

I lead Kristyna out of the chaos. We're quite the sight. She's wearing what was once a white dress but, with my hand in the middle of her back, there's now blood streaming down it. Meanwhile my grey suit is splattered with blood and to top it off I'VE SPLIT MY PANTS.

This is the classic Perkins paradox: the best and worst of me together in the same moment. Defending a loved one by vanquishing an evildoer but going so far over the top that I'm left looking and feeling like a lunatic.

In the course of all the carnage two more of those stupid pointy statues went missing. They weren't stolen. It's just that I forgot to take them amid all the chaos. One was left stabbed into the wall. Another, pocketed

by other people. Three remained in possession of the group. Actually, I'm not sure where they ended up either.

Days later someone sends a photo of one of our ARIAs to Triple J and offers to give it back . . . but only if I turn up at their place naked. They also demand that James Cruickshank be reinstated into the band. James hadn't been with us at the ARIAs so this ransom demander assumed he wasn't in the band anymore. James *was* still in the band, but he'd just got out of hospital after a car accident while driving under the influence of heroin and had gone straight back to using, so we thought it best he stayed home that night.

This was the top of the mountain.

This was success.

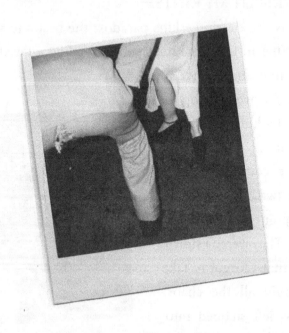

FLYING HIGH

The ARIA debacle also left me with another painful legacy I live with — or is that, limp with? — to this day.

It was about two weeks after the ARIA Awards night and the record company wanted me to go to Europe to do a week of interviews. This was at the height of The Cruel Sea's success so I go Business Class.

Ooooooh yeeeeah. Business Class, oh Business Class how I love thee, I want to die in Business Class, oh my dear darling business class ... ah hm ... Sorry.

Anyway, so here I am in Business Class on this long flight and I'm sitting next to this other young fella who turns out to be an actor on the *Home and Away*. I'd never seen him before but that's what he said he did so who was I to argue? He says he's off to England to do the appearance circuit. I ask what that is and he explains that all he's got to do is turn up at various nightclubs, get up onstage, talk to the DJ for a few minutes, chat to a few people then walk out with a thousand pounds. LADIES AND GENTLEMEN WOULD YOU WELCOME THIS GEEZER FROM *HOME AND AWAY!*

Anyway, we're drinking and enjoying ourselves. Enjoying all the goodies of BUSINESS CLASS. Our drink of choice on this flight is champagne and vodka – in the same glass. A Vodka Royale is the name of the concoction. We get pretty pissed pretty quickly. Then I decide to have a look at what's in my Business Class pack – and among other things there's cabin socks. They're these socks you put over your socks, probably to contain the foot odour. So I think, 'Okey dokey, I'll put my cabin socks on.' That's what you do in Business Class. You wear cabin socks.

The flight goes on. The drinking goes on. Not much sleeping goes on. More drinking goes on. There's probably only a couple of hours to go before we get to London and the actor and I are hanging back near the kitchen area, drinking and chatting to another passenger.

I feel like a little walk and there in front of me is a carpeted staircase up to FIRST CLASS so I decide that I'll go for a wander up there and see what First Class is all about. I get up these carpeted stairs, have a look down the aisle and decide that it doesn't look much better than where I am and it's boring, so I start to descend the staircase – this carpeted staircase – in my cabin socks.

Then I slip and bounce all the way to the bottom, landing in an awkward position and completely fucking my knee. It's absolutely excruciating. I've actually done the sort of injury that footballers do – torn a meniscus cartilage. And I'm in absolute agony, lying in a twisted heap at the bottom of the First Class stairs. The *Home and Away* actor jumps to my aid. 'I'm fucked,' I say in a loud grimacing whisper. Someone from the cabin crew runs over, grabs the mic and does the classic 'Is there a doctor onboard?' announcement.

And yes, there is a doctor onboard and he comes to look at me.

His prognosis: I *am* fucked.

They need to find somewhere to lay me out and so they take me to the cabin crew's private napping area and put me on one of their beds and the doctor tells me to take off my pants as he needs to have a look at my knee. Even through the agony I have the foresight to tell him, 'I'm not wearing any under-pants.' The *Home and Away* guy says that I can borrow a spare pair of his and runs off to get me a pair of Calvin Klein undies from his man bag.

My knee is swollen to a ridiculous size now and we have just under two hours before we land in London. And then I'm due to catch a connecting flight to Paris.

I'm still in excruciating pain and when we land they put me in a wheelchair and I'm rolled onto my connecting flight. In Paris I'm met by a bewildered record company rep who reports back to the record company that *the talent is broken*, and we should just cancel this publicity tour and turn me around and send me home.

'No, I'm here now, I'm doing it, I just need help,' I say. So they take me to my hotel room but we should've gone straight to hospital. I was in incredible pain all night. The next day at the hospital, the frog doctor put rows of needles in my grotesquely swollen knee and drained it of a whole lot of bloody fluid. Each needle spouting blood like an oil well. All this time I'm still wearing the soap actor's undies.

I hobbled around Europe on crutches for a week. And I've been hobbling a little ever since. I've never had an operation to get in there and fix it properly so it's still kinda twisted and damaged and getting worse with age.

But I'm okay.

I try not to fall down stairs these days.

I don't drink Vodka Royales.

I never, ever take off my shoes on a plane.

But I'll never, ever blame Business Class.

ONE FOR THE ROAD(IE)

In the mid '90s The Cruel Sea were in Europe.

It was a typical tour. You do the gig and then you pile into the bus with all the food and booze left over from the backstage rider and off you go. That's how you exist on tours like this. You get on the bus, drink and carry on for a while then crawl into your bunk and fall asleep while the driver drives through the night to the next gig and when you wake up you're either in the next town or at least well on your way to getting there.

Travelling by bus was more cost-effective than paying for hotel rooms every night and flying between gigs. It becomes a routine. You fall into the rhythm of it and before you know it you're used to this grubby little way of life.

Tonight it's Bill the bus driver – we never knew his last name, he never needed one – and he's driving all night and we're all asleep in our bunks going from Madrid to Lisbon.

At around six or seven in the morning Bill stops at a truck stop and goes in for a shit and a truckie's breakfast. Meanwhile we're all slowly waking up and one by one we all stagger off the bus to take a piss or get a coffee.

Now, at this particular truck stop things are divided into two sections. There's the truckers' section which is where Bill is, and then there's everybody else's section which is where we go. You can't see one section from the other.

What happens next is Bill finishes his breakfast and morning ablutions and happily gets back on the bus, looks down the aisle and sees that everything looks to be as it was – it's still quiet so everyone's still sleeping soundly, and he turns on the engine and starts driving the rest of the way to Lisbon. *Without anybody else on the bus.*

We're all still having our cups of tea or coffee wearing whatever we slept in, some of us with no shoes on, most of us with no wallets or ID.

Bill meanwhile is driving ALL THE WAY to Lisbon thinking we're just a bit quiet today.

Only when he arrives in Lisbon and presumably calls out to everyone to wake up does he realise that we're not on the bus. Not the band. Not the crew. Not the manager. No one.

This was around 1994 so there were no mobile phones or anything like that. So instead we just sat around waiting – FOR SIX FUCKING HOURS. Earlier in the tour somebody had mentioned that there were bandits out our way and that it was not uncommon for car-jackings or indeed bus-jackings to take place. So we're thinking that Bill's had his throat cut and been thrown in a ditch somewhere. And to be honest, by the time he got back some six hours later we kinda wished he had been.

When he finally returned, Bill the bastard thought it was funny, which I suppose it is, now. But certainly not at the time.

A band isn't just made up of the blokes who walk onstage. There have been many gentlemen and gentlewomen of the road over the years – fine human beings all – that have tuned our guitars, driven our vans, carried our equipment and put up with all our bullshit.

But it all began with Speedy.

Speedy (real name Peter Dick) was from Brisbane and came onto the scene about the

Speedy at breakfast.

same time as I did. When I met him he had just started working for The Johnnys. Speedy just turned up to one of their early shows in Brisbane and asked if he could help out. By the end of the night he had made himself indispensable and when they left Brisbane, he went with them.

Speedy had flaming red hair shaved into a mohawk. He was strong as a bull and keen and loyal as a kelpie. In those early days Speedy worked for lots of different bands but would always find time for The Johnnys and The Beasts Of Bourbon. He loved us. And we loved him.

Speedy enjoyed his reputation for being an almost psychic roadie. It seemed like he would be there not just after the guitar player broke a string but just *before* the string broke. He was amazing.

He also had a reputation for being able to eat . . . anything. When he and the Beasts arrived in Europe in 1989, we immediately went to McDonald's so Speedy could eat – I kid you not – seven Big Macs. When we ate together Speedy would always clean everybody else's plates of any leftovers. The boy needed fuel!

This of course led to a hubris involving his ability to consume many, many beers as well, and this of course led to many, many 'adventures'.

One night Speedy got very drunk at a bar in some town in deepest darkest Switzerland and couldn't find his way back to the hotel. After walking around in circles, lost for some time, he decided to ask for help at the local police station. Unable to even remember the name of the hotel Speedy gave the police no choice but to lock him up in a cell for the night. This suited Speedy just fine. In the morning he walked out the front door of the police station to see our hotel directly opposite the cop shop.

'Morning Speedy,' we said as we loaded the van and drove on.

Speedy got beat up by the Queensland coppers packing up after a gig on the Gold Coast one night.

'What's your name son?'

'Speedy.'

WHACK!

'WHAT'S YOUR REAL NAME SON?!'

'Dick.'

WHACK!

'One last chance smart arse, what's your name?'

'Peter Dick sir.'

WHACK! ZAM! POW!

Years full of hundreds of gigs and thousands of beers followed, but somewhere along the way Speedy's hijinks became less funny. Drunk as a monk he once drove the truck with the PA and all our equipment in it into a ditch somewhere and then walked away unable to remember where he'd left it. Something had happened in his private life and his excesses now had a darkness to them. Whole bottles of vodka disappeared around Speedy.

One morning in 1996 he was found dead in front of the TV in his flat in Brisbane. He had taken home the rider of some band he was working for the night before. Some band that didn't drink much. I guess he thought a slab of VB, a bottle of vodka and a hit of heroin was a good way to wind down after a hard day's night.

Speedy, gentleman of the road, worked hard, went hard and died hard.

In truth, the road crew were often the most interesting dudes around. The Cruel Sea had a crew that were cooler than the band; Kelvin, Cloth Ears and the Mook were much more attractive and always had a lot more fun than us. All those guys are still alive but a lot of fellas of that profession didn't make it. The suicide rate is a frightening five times the national average.

It's not a coincidence that rock'n'roll and the military both use the term 'tours'. Long tours can change people, and when they return to civilian life they can find it hard to fit back into the real world. Without the routine and the support and camaraderie of their on-the-road family, they feel lost and adrift.

The Cruel Sea had a tour manager during the '90s who tried to tip the balance back towards the crew. Howard Freeman, or 'The Bald Guy' as he liked to be known, was like a football coach or a drill sergeant. He loved his crews and they loved him. But he hated us. Hated musicians in general. Thought we were all big self-indulgent, self-destructive babies. He was right.

ZONE BALL

Another legacy of the road is road games.

Anyone who spends much time around me knows I'm competitive. Now when people say 'you're competitive', there seems to be an assumption that you're a poor sport and hate to lose. Which couldn't be further from the truth. I like games. I like to compete. I like to feel challenged in that way. I don't mind losing, just as long as it's been a good contest. In fact I'd prefer to compete well but ultimately lose. After all, I'm a Saint.

I'm a bit of a gamesman and always have been. Games like darts and pool and ping pong can make a long, arduous tour tolerable.

Zone Ball came about because usually an Aussie Rules football would accompany the bands on tour, especially the Dark Horses and The Cruel Sea. (The Beasts Of Bourbon have never been a footy band. Everybody's always been too hungover to even think about activities involving coordination.)

Often we'd find ourselves indoors, in empty rooms, pubs or arenas, where we couldn't really have a proper kick. But we'd have a go. Someone would bring out the footy to kill time before or after sound check, but space was an issue.

It's weird how things evolve. One day we were just aimlessly kicking a ball around when someone started catching it one-handed. The idea came to try one-handed marks. And through activities like this you start putting boundaries and rules in place and before you know it you're designing this game.

That's how Zone Ball started. Nothing planned. Just a case of working out a game that we could play with elements of footy but in a small space.

Zone Ball is a cross between football and tennis, and it's played between two people. In essence you 'serve' the football into an area you imagine as being like a tennis court. One person kicks or serves the footy into the zone and the other person has to mark it one-handed. There's a lot of rules but basically it's kicking into the other player's zone but making it difficult for them to mark it. And it has to be a one-handed mark.

Over time we developed and refined more and more rules for Zone Ball. Increasingly people heard about it. Over the 12 or 13 years since I first started it up there have been small flurries of interest where it's felt like it's almost going to take that next step into being a legitimate sport, which is a bit of a joke. I mean, the one-handedness of it was really because at the time we were probably holding a cigarette or a beer or a joint – maybe juggling all three and trying to play with the footy.

In fact, Zone Ball actually threatened to go legit when Western Bulldogs captain Bob Murphy devoted a whole column in *The Age* to it.

Bob explained other things about the game – how opposing players must bow to each other before the start and at the completion of every match, for example. He also pointed out that if your serve lands outside the court, this is defined as a 'bad', and if there's two 'bads' in a row a point is conceded. If a 'bad' is marked – one-handed of course – that's a score of two points. A 'shocker' is when a serve fails to leave the server's zone, and is worth two points. A 'big, bad shocker' is when your opponent marks the ball in your zone. Such a feat is rare and therefore worth three points. There are many, many more rules, but the above maybe gives you an idea.

I've developed other games. There's one called Slidey which is perfect for rock'n'roll bands killing time backstage in a dressing room before or after a gig.

Slidey is basically where you slide bottles across a table and try to get the bottle as close as possible to the edge without it going over. It's best played with beer bottles. But wine bottles or really any object will do. It's fundamentally like bowls – but played with bottles . . . on a table.

In lots of ways all this is symptomatic of the daily grind and life of travelling rock'n'roll bands, who have no real choice but to develop games with whatever's at hand to fill in time.

TEX

With no regular access to a billiard table or a pool table or a ping pong table you kind of make up games out of whatever is around you.

Games, they're good for brain.

ROOM SERVICE

I love hotel rooms.

My sanctuary. My cell. My tomb.

Just kidding.

Hotels are one of the constants in the life of any touring musician. And I've spent a LOT of nights in hotel rooms. Now listen, I may have been a rock star in the classic mould, but I've never been a TV-out-the-window kinda guy . . . well, not that I can remember anyway. Sure, things have been broken, and messes have been made. After all, drunk people have accidents. But I've never been a wilful-destruction-of-property kind of guy. Really, I'm not. Believe me.

In the late '90s, I was staying in my favourite boutique hotel of the time, just near Kings Cross. I'd been there for a week, working late and sleeping in and hadn't let housekeeping in for quite a while so the place was a real mess. I woke up on the last morning I was staying there and went to the Tropicana Caffe for breakfast, which was just across the road. After having my coffee and a tuna, cheese and tomato focaccia, I looked at the time and realised I was running late for the airport.

I ran back to my room, burst in the door and started throwing things in my bag. Halfway through the pack I put my bag up on the kitchen bench-top and ran into the bedroom and bathroom to get whatever was left in there. It must have taken me no more than three minutes, but when I returned to the lounge/kitchen area I was surprised to see the room was filled with smoke! WHAT THE?! I looked around to see my bag was on fire! I had accidentally pushed my bag onto the stovetop and knocked the switch on FULL. I threw the bag into the nearby kitchen sink to extinguish the inferno, smashing plates and glasses in the process. FAARRRK. I don't have time for this!

Amazingly, neither the fire alarm nor the sprinkler system was activated. I grabbed my wet but still smouldering bag, now with a great gaping hole in the bottom, to my body so the contents wouldn't fall out and ran out of the room. A big puff of smoke followed me out as the door closed behind. The lift seemed to take forever, but luckily it came empty. When I arrived on the ground floor I was met by Steve, the very enthusiastic fellow at reception.

'GOOD MORNING, MR PERKINS! GOOD MORNING! LET ME TAKE YOUR BAG!'

'Oh no, no thanks I'm fine,' I said, clutching it tighter to my body as the smell of burnt sports bag surely filled the room. 'I'm running a bit late for the airport.'

'PLEASE LET ME TAKE YOUR BAG.'

'No no no, please I'm fine, here's my key, thank you.'

'THEN LET ME HAIL YOU A CAB.'

'Ummm ... err.'

Steve, bless him, stood out there for five minutes chatting with me until a taxi whisked me away from the scene of the crime. I never heard a word about it. Another clean getaway.

Sure, as I said, things get broken, busted and burnt but believe me, I meant no harm. I never made a mess just for the fun of it ... really, I wouldn't, it's not my ... well there was that one time.

We were staying in the motel section of some beer barn we'd played in the mid-'90s. So after the show our drinks rider gets dragged into my nearby room, and a small party breaks out with the band, crew and some of the punters.

At some stage a girl produces a bunch of glow sticks, the kind full of fluorescent fluid. She punctures one end so the fluid leaks out. Then like a magic wand starts flicking the glow stick at the wall, splattering it in fluid. With the lights on you couldn't really notice anything, but when the lights were turned off, ZING! A startling splash of fluorescent lime-green splatter. Everyone immediately grabbed a stick and started splattering – everything. We quickly reached the point of no return, and went way beyond it. No point in stopping now. It was a spectacular display – the entire motel room covered in a fluorescent green Jackson Pollock.

Next morning in the daylight you couldn't really notice the fluid on the walls. But apparently when the elderly couple that checked in two days later turned off the lights for a good night's rest? Well, they noticed.

TouRING WITH THE STONES

I was a bit of a cheeky prick at the time The Cruel Sea toured with the Rolling Stones.

It was the Voodoo Lounge tour of Australia in March 1995.

As much as I love the Rolling Stones – so many great tunes, so much mythology, they are for me THE greatest band of all time and have given me more joy, more pleasure, more inspiration than anyone else – by this stage they had been making a lot of shit records for many years so I was a bit blasé about the whole thing.

The whole SHOW that they put on is stadium entertainment – lots of running from one side of an enormous stage to the other. Over-the-top gestures and a ridiculous amount of lights, screens and special effects.

But the coolest thing was seeing their sound checks, where they just played music – no show, no bullshit, just them playing their songs to themselves. They played songs at sound checks that weren't in the show; songs that their massive audience of people who come to just one rock concert a year wouldn't care to hear. Things like 'I Got The Blues' and Keith's 'You Got The Silver'. It was heaven.

So yes, it was extremely cool to get to tour with the Rolling Stones but I was a little, well, *loose* with my respect on the tour.

For starters, The Cruel Sea were really given the 'support band treatment'. Some people have even suggested that we went on *before* the gates were open and people were let in. That's not true, but as you'd expect we played while people were coming in and finding their seats. We weren't surprised when it happened. We were in awe of our surroundings, but some nights I couldn't help myself. Once after we finished I said to the crowd, 'Don't go home ladies and gentlemen, there's another band on after us.'

Then I upped it a bit the next night with, 'Ladies and gentlemen, next on . . . The Beatles.'

I'm not sure whether any of the Stones heard this. Probably not. But it felt like maybe Keith did. We were backstage one night in this area they called the Voodoo Lounge which was like a really extended Green Room. It had a huge food buffet with couches and TVs and the latest pub-style video games. One of which was a favourite of mine at the time – *Daytona*. Jim Elliot and I, having just finished a race were standing near the machine.

Enter Mick Jagger.

'Ello lads ow ya doin, aw rite?'

'Yeah man, how are you? Just enjoying the facilities.'

'*Daytona* ay? Fancy a race?'

'Fuck yeah!' I said, pushing in front of Jim and sitting back down in one of the driver's seats. Everything was free, so away we went. Me and Mick.

Mick fumbled with the gear stick and steering wheel, meandering all over the virtual racetrack. Realising how awful he was, I slowed down and tried not to completely destroy him, but he made it very difficult for me to do a convincing job. 'He spent a lot of money getting that good on that machine,' Jim said comfortingly to Mick as we stood up after the race.

Perkins 1, Jagger 0.

There was a full-size billiard table for Ronnie and Keith and they seemed to have a game before very show.

On another night, I wandered over to the table to watch them play and I noticed that Ronnie was quite good and Keith was quite terrible. I felt uncomfortable and regretted coming over as Keith pushed the balls around the table with no results. No one likes onlookers when they're playing badly.

It was a rainy day and there was no cover on the stage. I asked the WAY too obvious question of 'what happens when it rains' and Keith looked at me and sneers, 'You get wet'.

Ronnie, attempting to lighten the mood, pipes up with a cheery, 'Once in Rio we were playing in a raging hurricane and the rain was coming in horizontally, but we played on. Nothing stops the Stones.'

Jagger was professionally friendly. He was like a politician in that he has a little bit of information on everyone so it seems like he remembers you and cares. He said he'd been listening to our current album and went on to describe a couple of aspects of it, trying to make us feel good, and it did, bless him. But nothing prepared me for how little they all were – I mean they were tiny. They were like miniatures. It seemed like they couldn't have been much more than five foot tall! Jim and I are both around six foot four; we felt weird towering over these giants of rock.

Some people thought it was a bit of a coup for us to get that tour and I suppose it was. On the other hand, I think they just got the biggest band in the country at the time and that just happened to be The Cruel Sea. Six months later it would have been Silverchair.

YOU'RE HIM, ARENT YA?

Certainly there's been times when I've been rude to people.

And I'm sorry for that. Really I am. But I give as good as I get. You give someone some time but then they want a bit more. It's going well, so they just want to take a little bit more, and they can see that their time is really almost up so they throw in something that's a bit much and you say to them, 'Okay, that's enough, I've got to run now, bye', and as you walk off to catch your flight they say something like, 'I always knew you were a wanker.'

It's like that scene in *The King Of Comedy* where Jerry Lewis is walking along the street and people are cheering and applauding him, they're coming up to him and he's signing autographs, and then this old Jewish woman comes up, and he signs an autograph for her and as she's gushing with compliments she asks for something else and he says, 'Sorry I have to go now.' And she yells at him, 'GET CANCER! YOU SHOULD GET CANCER!!'

The people I encounter are not usually that extreme but that sort of reaction – to varying degrees – is a very common phenomenon. They come on to you and they get your attention and then they want to see how far they can stretch it. They're not happy until they've pushed it as far as they can.

Big Day Out, 1994. Notice the sign stuck to my back; I think it said KICK ME.

Most people are really lovely. Australia, you should be proud of yourself, statistically speaking you're ALL RIGHT.

But of course there's the – often well-meaning – clowns who walk past and go 'BETTER GET A LAWYER – BETTER GET A GOOD ONE.' That happens a lot.

My favourite is the guy – and it's usually a guy – who comes up and goes, 'You're him, fuck me, seriously, are you him?'

'Umm, I dunno mate.' I mean does he think I'm Tim Rogers? Nick Cave? Gary Aires?

'I saw you supporting the Stones in '95 at the MCG', and you think to yourself, *Good on you mate, that was 25 years ago.*

You have a keen eye and a sharp memory. Thanks for telling me. I really feel like we have a connection. We should have lunch.

There's a common misconception that does the rounds and that I hear a lot. It pretty much goes that every guy wants to *be me* and every woman wants to *do me*. Yeah, I know, it's creepy, isn't it?

In 2010 a band called ROOT! recorded a song called 'I Wish I Was Tex Perkins', about the atmosphere of envy that follows me. People around me thought I would be offended. But the only issue I had with the song was that it wasn't funny enough.

Let's sort all that out, shall we?

The actual equation is that guys come up to me at gigs, usually after a few drinks and they get up close in my face and sneer, 'My girlfriend thinks you're hot. My GIRLFRIEND LOVES YOU.' They're talking through gritted teeth. 'MY GIRLFRIEND FUCKING LOVES YOU ... AND IT'S REALLY GOOD TO MEET YOU.'

I try to keep sweet with these guys for as long as possible but sure enough it turns weird, and occasionally nasty, especially if it's in a pub, which it usually is.

The guy will eventually turn sour. I can see it coming. They're slurring by this stage and not totally sure on their footing. 'MY GIRLFRIEND THINKS YOU'RE SEXY ...' They go on and on.

I can see them looking me up and down and thinking to themselves, *What the fuck does she see in YOU? Has she had a good look at YOU?*

Usually, after the fourth or fifth time they've told me that their girlfriend thinks I'm hot, I say, 'Well, you can go back to her now and say it's all been a terrible mistake.'

THREE LEGGED DOG

A wise man once said: 'There's a difference between scratching your arse and ripping it to shreds.'

This could be applied to many things but it's especially true of fame. Our society is geared towards having more, all the time more, more, MORE. Bigger is better and biggest is best. Even though the evidence is undeniable, I know most of you will never believe me when I say that a little bit of fame is great but a lot of it is almost always bad.

These days a fast track to the big time is always favoured over longevity, balance and sustainability.

I like the level of fame where the waiter at the restaurant is a little friendlier when they're serving you, rather than the level of fame where they clear everyone else from the restaurant so you can eat alone. Minor fame is fun and easy to handle and has a few perks. Huge fame is when you need to create a world separate from everyday life and have the money and power to do that (think Michael Jackson). Then there's the level just below that where you're up there but also *out there* exposed to the onslaught (think Kurt Cobain).

I'm not sure why I was a little predisposed for this life I've led, being an awkward loner of a child with an instinct for performance. But I've also never been far from someone who'd remind me that my physical appearance wasn't to their liking. From, 'Why is he so skinny? Doesn't he eat?' from my grandmother, to my footy coach's mournful assessment, 'Look at that long streak of pelican shit.'

As a geeky kid I wondered what it would be like to be an attractive person or even just a person that didn't feel like people were pointing and laughing at them, but when I finally was looked at for the 'right' reasons, it was excruciatingly uncomfortable. What some people read as arrogance, is really defensive, as deep down I assume I'm being attacked, put down or written off.

Pretty much straight after *The Honeymoon Is Over* was released it dawned on The Cruel Sea that we *were* on to something here. At that moment of realisation some of the most significant members of the band started getting spooked by the success. Most significantly me and Danny – not together, but separately – started to question it.

Once we had decided to make 'commercial' music, success had happened too quickly, too easily and so I sort of didn't respect it. I was suspicious. It seemed too easy. The carry-on about how great we were just didn't wash. And the pressure that came with success didn't make me comfortable. Our climb up the ladder of success made us feel like now we just had a higher place to fall from. The back lash could arrive any minute now.

Danny had his own issues. I think he felt his music was being compromised. Danny was never quite satisfied that the band captured the magic of his original demos. And that's true – those demo recordings were unique. But this was something different now. Danny struggled with what was going on. He became more insular and cut himself off from the rest of the band, often choosing to travel with the support band or the crew rather than us.

This was the unhappiest time of the band's life.

We went through this maelstrom for 18 months until it was of course time to make another album. Then there was an almost deliberate attempt to dismantle what we had built. That album was *Three Legged Dog* and even the title was an intentional turn off, designed to elicit a feeling that was a bit weird and difficult and unpleasant. The music itself was more stripped back and heavy and not as nice or appealing as *Honeymoon*.

It was important for us to make this statement at the time. I realise many of you will not believe me when I say that we wanted LESS success. But it was true. *Three Legged Dog* was an autobiographical album – a deliberate move to reclaim ownership of the band from the radio playlists and public-image purveyors. It was our attempt to pull the band back from being this mainstream thing that could appear on *Hey Hey It's*

Saturday and be loved by all. We were battered and bruised – half of us were literally on crutches – and wanted to apply a handbrake to our runaway success.

And it WORKED. We halved our sales. But we halved the pressure too.

THREE LEGGED DOG

THE CRUEL SEA / 1995

Probably this took about three weeks all up, in two
different studios with Paul McKercher and Tony Cohen.
The name of the album was a working title, referring to
the state of the band at the time. Both James and I were
on crutches when we started recording at Rocking Horse
Studios in Byron. It was the first album we began pre-
production on with nothing in the pot. All of Danny's
demos had been exhausted, and we started from scratch
and wrote most of it as a band. A deliberate attempt to
wrestle back ownership of our success, it's a loose and
dirty record, designed to not win any ARIA awards.
Despite our best efforts, it got us the best band award
and still sold Platinum.

RECORD LABEL: *Red Eye*
CORE BAND MEMBERS: *Tex Perkins (vocals), Danny Rumour (guitar),
Jim Elliot (drums), Ken Gormley (bass), James Cruikshank (keyboards/guitar).*

Serenading my hand on stage with the *Beasts*.

Courtesy Tony Mott

Big Day Out, 1994.

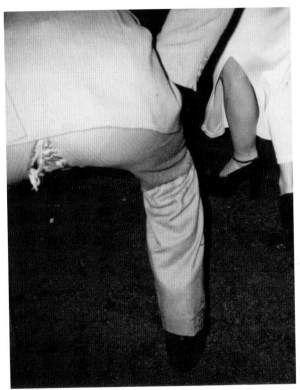

Following the fight at the ARIAs - if you can tear your eyes away from the split in my pants, note the blood on the cuff of my trousers.

The Cruel Sea, backstage in Europe, 1994.

Me and Kristyna, sometime in the years before
parenthood, when we had time to lollygag
in photobooths.

Big Day Out, January 1993. My daughter Tuesday, me,
Mark Arm (Mudhoney), Kim Gordon (Sonic Youth), Iggy Pop
and Nick Cave (Bad Seeds). Great times. A lot of people draw
comparisons between me and Cavo, but this photo clearly shows
the difference between us, he in his $400 Italian silk number and
me in my buttonless miller shirt tied together with a rag.
He's all forehead and I'm no forehead. I'm ape-like and he's more
Herman Munster. Note also the unlit cigarette in my mouth.
It's around the wrong way. I didn't even smoke . . . cigarettes.

Spencer Jones:
something to
lean on.

Beasts by
name ...
At Big Day Out
in 2006. This
was one of our
first return
gigs after Brian
broke his back.
From left to
right is
Spencer, Brian,
Tony, me and
Charlie.

Me and Iggy, mirroring each other with our highly choreographed dance routine, 1993.

Me and Tim Rogers, lost in a moment together.

Me conducting The
Bumhead Orchestra
like a highly
emotional traffic
controller, at
Big Day Out 2006.

The Ladyboyz (arguably the nation's fifth best covers band) and Adalita performing 'You and Me' in 2008.

The 2014 'Save the Palais' campaign: me and the old girl.

The Far From Folsom concerts, where I sang Johnny Cash in old prisons around Australia.

Thank you and goodnight.

RAP - MY PART IN ITS DOWNFALL

'Better Get a Lawyer', the first single from *Three Legged Dog*, was much more than a song; it was a deliberate step away from the sound people knew us for.

It was also when my love for rap and hip hop found full expression. Let me explain.

At first I would only rap when I was being silly, taking the piss at a rehearsal for The Cruel Sea or The Beasts Of Bourbon. But slowly, as rap and hip hop became more widespread, it felt more and more natural to slip it in . . . a little here, a little there.

When I was recording the album *This Is Not The Way Home* with The Cruel Sea, the song 'Don't Sell It' had a section that doubles up the rhythm that was perfect for me to break into a rap run tightly together. In the end I used the entire lyrics of 'Straight Hard and Long', a Beasts song I'd written in 1991. It worked, sort of.

By the time *Three Legged Dog* came along, Beck had become a good example of how a white boy should rap and the songs 'Better Get a Lawyer' and 'Too Fast For Me' carried rapped stanzas inspired by his influence.

The first hip hop I'd ever heard was Blondie's 'Rapture'. Deborah Harry's rapping was cute, but it was approached (by the band and the critics) as a novelty. I mean Blondie had done reggae, disco and punk rock. They were just playing. It wasn't the instant cultural shift you might expect considering where hip hop has ended up. But 'Rapture' did bring rock-loving kids from the suburbs like me to the art form and introduced it to the mainstream as a basic blueprint a lot of modern music has utilised since.

After 'Rapture', the next thing I heard was 'The Message' by Grandmaster Flash. . . . Now this sounded serious! The music was funky as fuck and the lyrics were great. It wasn't only the lyrics, it was the *way* they were delivered and the heavy wisdom of it all. It reminded me of Stevie Wonders 'Livin' For The City' – it had the sound of the street in it. Literally, as they both had recorded street sounds of traffic and sirens.

Eighties acts like Tone Lōc, LL Cool J, Salt-N-Pepa and Run DMC represented hip hop to the casual listener. Enjoyable, but unimportant – to me anyway. But James Brown and George Clinton samples mixed with discordant tape loops? *That* was an exciting new sound.

Towards the end of the decade, things got *really* interesting.

It's always a good sign when you hear about a group before you actually hear them. The first time I heard people discussing Public Enemy they talked about them like they were ISIS. Here was a black militant rap group urging an uprising from black people EVERYWHERE. Their song titles alone – 'Don't Believe The Hype', 'Louder Than A Bomb', 'Bring The Noise', and 'Fight The Power' – caused anxiety and concern. Like Grand Master Flash, Public Enemy's music was heavy but extremely funky. Irresistibly danceable. Best of all, it had a revolutionary vibe that was utterly convincing and sweeping the world, which scared a lot of God-fearing white folks – well, mainly parents and cops – even in Australia.

Today hip hop is so mainstream and so disgustingly bloated and self-congratulatory it's probably more 'rock'n'roll' than rock'n'roll ever was – in a very bad way. In fact, with its love of wealth and power it's far more in need of a kick in the teeth than rock was in the '70s. Back then punk rock came and did that job. But I fear nothing can stop hip hop now. These days I can't stand most rap. The hip hop I listen to, things like DJ Shadow and Cut Chemist, is instrumental. And if I start rapping, slap me.

GONE

THE BEASTS OF BOURBON / 1997

I have no idea how long this took, probably about two
weeks. This one's a real mess, but it was meant to be.
I sacked Tony halfway through this record for stealing
things from the studio. Paul McKercher took over and
steered and stirred this unpleasant brew of bile until
it resembled something like music. This was Charlie's
first record with the Beasts, and if people didn't like this
album they tended to blame him. Charlie bore the brunt
of the 'they're no good without Kim' naysayers. But I've
noticed over the years a small but passionate group of
degenerates around the world love this album. Perhaps
they recognise themselves.

RECORD LABEL: *Polydor*
CORE BAND MEMBERS: *Tex Perkins (vocals), Spencer P. Jones (guitar),
Charlie Owen (guitar), Brian Hooper (bass), Tony Pola (drums).*

CHASING
THE DRAGON

Drugs are everywhere in rock'n'roll — as they are in life.

I've tried them all, well, not ALL of them, but let's say I'm experienced in this area. But as a wise man once said, 'there's a difference between scratching your arse and ripping it to shreds.' I like pot. I've always liked pot and I probably always will. It's not only a wonder drug, as day by day we find out more about how wonderful and beneficial it is to a lot of people, but it's also a wonder plant. We could save the world with this weed, as it can be used to make everything from clothes to biodegradable plastics. But let's talk about the hard stuff. Using drugs can lead to crazed desperate behaviour, manic delusions and an inflated belief in one's own abilities.

But there's also a downside.

Some people handle drugs well and actually thrive creatively while using them. Others aren't so lucky and either rapidly or slowly kill themselves. Often I think it has a lot to do with genetics. Some people are preconditioned to cope with massive punishment from drugs and booze, cruising through bender after bender as if bulletproof.

In the '80s I don't think I knew anyone who didn't drink more than they should and take as many drugs as they could get their hands on. The '90s were no different – except some people seemed to have a bit more money to buy more and better drugs. Some people forgot the better part and just bought more – and more – and more.

From about 1984 to 1999 every band I was in had junkies in it. Okay, *junkie* might be a harsh word to use – let's call them heavy habitual users of heroin. Better?

In the beginning, a guy like Stu Spasm would drop on a very regular basis. We'd slap him around, throw him in the bath and he'd wake up and complain, 'Why am I all wet?'

For a certain period of The Beasts Of Bourbon in the early to mid-'90s – just after Kim Salmon left and was replaced by Charlie Owen – there was heroin everywhere.

As I've detailed, The Beasts Of Bourbon were true beasts when it came to drugs. Nobody ever said 'you've got to stop taking this drug, it's not good for you'. But after a decade of debauchery, a few of us really started to fuck up. We had to cancel a huge European tour because Spencer OD'd a few days before we were meant to leave. On this particular night he was brought back from the brink of death by a fast-acting bandmate who gave him cardiac resuscitation. Unfortunately, the pressured chest-thumping from the CPR burst an ulcer in Spencer's fetid gut which put him in hospital for a few weeks. It wasn't the first or last time that Spencer's hubris about his ability to consume drugs would lead to trouble.

In The Cruel Sea everybody maintained their own very personal habits, hiding it away from everybody else. No one was admitting to anything and everyone who was using was pretending they weren't. In the end, one by one, various people were forced to leave the band for six months at a time to try to get clean.

And then James Cruickshank fell asleep in his car driving on that flyway piece of road from Woollahra to the south end of Bondi. Cruikers had scored, fixed and set off to drive home to Bondi. He nodded off, went across three lanes and had a head-on collision with a truck. He was lucky – very lucky – that he didn't die right then and there. And also lucky he didn't kill the guy in the truck, or anyone else on the road for that matter. Shit was getting serious.

The Cruel Sea was a wreck of its own invention by that stage. But the show must go on. Danny had his own habit and typically would keep it very organised. He'd have his gear rationed out and he'd take just enough every time and keep it very private. Kenny had his own unique problems and was in and out of the band three times.

The general attitude in The Cruel Sea was lackadaisical – everyone was cool and could cope and do their own thing. But once Cruickshank had his head-on, it was obvious that things had to change. The secrecy was exposed. Some guys in the band would say adamantly, 'No, no, no, I'm not stoned, I'm just tired.' But denial can only take you so far.

With the Beasts it was all yahooing and carrying on, almost like a bunch of boy scouts with that 'one for all, all for one' camaraderie. Early incarnations of the Beasts hadn't been drug bands. They'd been almost totally fuelled on VB with a bit of speed thrown in.

As we got bigger our riders grew and grew. First it was just more beer, but then we started seeing bottles of vodka and whiskey on the table next to the Smiths Crisps. Then two bottles of vodka and three bottles of whiskey. Very soon the Beasts had the biggest drink rider in the business. Venues were happy to shell out because our audiences were always the biggest drinkers, so they were making a shitload over the bar. The junkie line-up of the Beasts came later. That's when it became a truly scary, dark and ugly rock'n'roll band. And despite everything, for the most part, we were still playing good.

But the best story about drugs I can remember didn't actually involve heroin – well not directly anyway. The Beasts were on tour in Europe in 2007. We had played the night before somewhere in France, but today we had to find Tony his medicine before we left town. That involved taking him to a GP and then the right pharmacist. A few hours later we're finally on our way to the next show in Zurich. Tony opens up his new packet of Subutex, which is some kind of synthetic morphine I guess.

'What does that stuff do?' someone casually asks.

'It makes me not need to score. Why don't you try one?'

'Errrr, I dunno.'

'Maybe just half then.'

'Okay.'

Someone else says, 'I'll have the other half.'

Feeling left out, I ask if I can have a quarter.

Feeling the generosity of a fat brand new packet Tony says 'sure'.

Half an hour later, I start to feel . . . pretty good, heeeeeey this is gonna be nice.

Ten minutes after that, I start to feel . . . REALLY BAD.

'Stop the van!' I quickly get out and throw up on the side of the autobahn.

I get back in and again we're under way.

STOP THE VAN!

Brian chunders his omelette all over the side rail.

He gets back in the van and WAIT, Spencer needs to yodel as well.

Get the picture? This went on for many kilometres, stopping every 20 minutes for someone, actually ALL of us to vomit, again and again.

When we finally arrived at the next gig we were in the worst state you could imagine. There, waiting for us at the back of the venue, were the promoter and all the venue's staff. The van finally came to rest and the doors burst open and the three of us leapt out and ran in different directions looking for places to vomit. This went on all night. During the gig Brian, Spencer and I had a garbage bin side of stage, which we would occasionally run off and barf into. 'I've just got to call my mother',

TEX

we would say as we darted off. Charlie and Tony thought it was hilarious, and it was. Well, it is, now.

I think the reason some of us did drugs was so we had funny stories to tell 20 years later. The Cruel Sea were in Amsterdam on tour supporting some guy known as the 'King of Goth' or something like that. It was a typical rock'n'roll tour. There were drugs of all descriptions everywhere. I never chased cocaine but if it was around . . . This was one of those occasions. There was coke everywhere in the backstage room. Everywhere.

So we go on and we do our set. It's stinking hot and I come off stage and head back into the room. The moment I sit down on the edge of the table there's silence in the room. Total silence. Everyone looks at me and then someone says, 'Get up very slowly – and then don't move.'

I've plonked myself down on seven lines of coke.

So I slowly prise myself off the table and stand up, and there stuck to the damp arse of my jeans are seven lines of coke. The next thing I know bank notes are being rolled up and one by one everyone in the room is coming over and snorting this coke off my arse.

But of course as things behind the scenes got messier, sometimes it spilled onto the stage too. Once, the Beasts played Hordern Pavilion. Now, the Hordern can be a bit of an echo chamber, a cavern . . . in fact more like the Grand Canyon as far as sound goes.

The Beasts are a band who cannot play unless the guitars are excruciatingly loud and on this night we're onstage and it's incredibly loud with echo and reverb. In situations like this I'm

238

very dependent on good monitors, otherwise I just can't hear what I'm doing or where I am in a song. So I'm out there trying to get through the gig and gesturing towards the monitor guys – UP, UP, UUUUUUUUPPP – to no avail and I'm getting more and more frustrated.

Tension builds. In the middle of the next song, I'm swamped in white noise but can't get the monitor guy's attention. I SNAP and pick up my microphone stand and javelin it across the stage and into the sound desk, scaring the shit out of the monitor guy.

This all happens in front of a whole lot of other Big Day Out bands watching from the side of the stage. Jerks like The John Spencer Blues Explosion who earlier in the day expressed their displeasure about having to go on before Dave Graney by sending their roadie on for a semi-naked stage invasion (being too New York to do it themselves).

I've heard other people tell their version of this story. One goes that I hit the monitor guy smack in the forehead and knocked him unconscious. People love to add those little extras. Little extras like attempted murder. But the fact is I did throw it and it did hit the desk. I had lost it completely and it was pretty disgraceful.

The best part though is when the gig finishes I'm still FUMING. I storm off stage and stomp upstairs to the dressing room. I get to the door and it's locked – I pace up and down for a few seconds not knowing what do. Then I turn around suddenly and attempt to kick the door open. Turns out the door is actually made out of little more than plywood and cardboard insulation and my foot goes straight through. Now I'm up to my knee in the door, suspended momentarily in that position.

In the next split second I decide to go through the door so I push my head and shoulders through and crash through in a hail of splinters and it's like one of those Warner Bros cartoons – there's just the outline of my full body in the door.

That's when Spencer comes along, turns the handle like a normal person and calmly opens the door with the Perko-shaped hole in it.

THE DEVIL'S MUSIC

Speaking of drugs and music let me say right here that I like the Eagles.

Thank you and goodnight.

Just kidding, but really, not many people in the rock scene that I inhabit will come out and say that. The idea that the Eagles are the epitome of boring overproduced middle-of-the-road '70s white-man rock is a cliché repeated by the same people who say Leonard Cohen is depressing and Bob Dylan can't sing. Sure, some of it is rather awful, but 'Witchy Woman' and 'One Of These Nights' are good examples what I would call the devil's music.

Yeah, I know that's supposed to be Robert Johnson and all that old blues stuff. But really, when you think about it, the devil's music is not gonna be dirty and lo fi. It's gonna be slick and shiny. It's gonna be as smooth as a dolphin's dick! It's gonna be in four-part harmonies and it's gonna slip into your soul in Dolby quadraphonic stereo sound.

All that '70s West Coast stuff. The Doobie Brothers, America, Fleetwood Mac, Joe Walsh, Linda Ronstadt, has a strange kind of darkness under its slick, clean surface. You know what I mean, maaaan? Flared pants, afros on white guys, cocaine and sunshine.

There's a sweetness to a lot of this music that's on the edge of turning. Like strawberry yoghurt in the sun. It's the soundtrack to the end of the hippy dream. The Stooges and Alice Cooper may take responsibility for the death of flower power, but the LA folkies were living its demise, and singing about it.

Of course, all those LA folkies were off their scones. By the mid-'70s there was a long tradition of fucked-up MOR folk pop singers. Jesus Christ, James Taylor made Keith Richards look like a lightweight. There's a reason his music is soooooo meloooooow. Smack.

Well actually apparently smack AND coke together. That's called a speed ball. The cocaine takes you up above the clouds and the smack is like a big soft pillow on the way down. All that West Coast stuff is dripping with burned-out drug comedown revelations.

Rumours by Fleetwood Mac is an incredible record, but when you know the legends of drug and relationship abuse surrounding that album it truly enhances the listening experience and gives the music another level of meaning – a depth beyond the music and lyrics of the songs.

Stevie Nicks' cocaine habit involving an assistant and a straw is now legendary.

You know what? When 'Hotel California' comes on the radio, I SING ALONG.

I drive my band mates nuts breaking into Little River Band tunes anywhere, anytime, harmonising for the fuck of it. Sure there is a touch of irony in my enjoyment of this kind of music. A tiny bit of taking the piss, but you can check out any time you like . . . oh and I also like Coldplay.

FAR BE IT FROM ME

TEX PERKINS / 1996

Ten days with Tony Cohen at Megaphon Studios in
Sydney. Charlie Owen, Jim White, Warren Ellis and I tried
to bring these songs to life. And I think we were partly
successful, but I don't know – there's something wrong
with this record. This is the first time I'd written without
irony or cynical humour. I wasn't used to it, and neither
was anybody else. This was an album written in a quiet
flat with a sleeping baby. It's about real love, not romantic
love; the dim glow of everyday love illuminates most of
these songs.

It ain't getting the kisses
It ain't getting your wishes
It's doing the dishes, that's real real love.

RECORD LABEL: *Polydor*
CORE BAND MEMBERS: *Tex Perkins (vocals), Charlie Owen (guitar),
Warren Ellis (strings/keyboards), Jim White (drums).*

OVER EASY

THE CRUEL SEA / 1998

Jeez, this is a strange piece of work. Broken up into a few small sessions and then a two-week stint at Rhino Studios in Sydney with Daniel Denholm and Phil McKellar, there are some good things on this but it's not a great record. At various times both Kenny and James were out of the band so it could've been called *Two Legged Dog*.

RECORD LABEL: *Polydor*
CORE BAND MEMBERS: *Tex Perkins (vocals), Danny Rumour (guitar), Jim Elliot (drums), Ken Gormley (bass), James Cruikshank (keyboards/guitar).*

GETTING MY SHIT TOGETHER

The Cruel Sea actually made money from record sales.

Most bands say they never make money from their album or CD sales, and that it all comes from live work and merchandise. And don't get me wrong; all record deals are an arse fuck, it's just by how much. Maybe we just got lucky, ours didn't go that deep.

To give you an idea of how good the money was, I bought my first piece of property, a flat in Melbourne, with cash. The more *The Honeymoon Is Over* sold the more my savings account grew – twenty grand here, fifty grand there. Most of the money was from record sales and, as a result of that, successful tours and while we were touring, successful merch sales. I ended up with upwards of three hundred grand just sitting in my savings account. That's when my friend and lawyer at the time, Bruno Charlesworth, told me that I should buy something solid.

I was living in Sydney at the time but even then it was frightening what everything cost. Then I noticed that in Melbourne you could buy something good for a couple of hundred thousand. Bruno took me for a drive around one day. I saw this place in Acland Street in St Kilda and literally said, 'I like this one', then I went and got the money out of the bank and paid for it. There was no need to ask for a loan. I had the money so it was mine to spend.

That place became my home base and at that point I moved to Melbourne for a couple of years. (I've still got it in fact.) With the collateral of that property, Kristyna and I stuck our necks out even further in 1997, buying a property in northern NSW. As I write these words, we're still there.

Initially this place was to be our country getaway and Melbourne would be the base, but we couldn't really afford to run two places so we moved up lock-stock in 1998.

That's how you do it, kids – you don't muck around. If you make a bit of money quickly you go out and buy something tangible. Preferably property.

By this time Kristyna and I had a family of our own. Scarlet was born in October 1995. Kristyna was astonishing. She owned that birth, with courage and raw power. It was like watching an Olympic event – easily the most powerful physical feat I've ever seen.

I was older and a little more ready than I had been with Tuesday five years

Parent Hood.

before, even becoming an expert with nappies. These were the cloth ones too, not the disposables. You had to fold it a certain way and secure it with a large safety pin without puncturing you or the baby.

Country life was a change in pace after the madness of touring with the Beasts and Cruel Sea, and I was more willing and able to embrace domesticity. It helped that Scarlet was a remarkable human, possessing the same intelligence, beauty and take-no-shit attitude as her mother. Ask anyone, Scarlet is hardcore.

Country life is sweet. To walk outside and eat something straight from the tree or the bush or even straight from the ground is a simple thing that brings me immense joy and satisfaction.

For me to see my children's faces smeared in mulberries or wild mango flesh is a wonderful thing to behold. And to collect your own water makes you keenly aware of what is taken for granted in the city. That certainly can be a pain in the arse at times but we live on the perimeter of social services so we have to deal with our own shit, literally.

That is also a very good philosophical standpoint. DEAL WITH YOUR OWN SHIT.

Society has become all too used to just flushing it away. Most people don't even look down as it goes; we just flush it away to somewhere else. Where? 'I don't care just as long as it's not here, just flush it on down the line, make it somebody else's problem.'

Our family uses a composting toilet much like one with plumbing, except you don't use litres and litres of water to get rid of your business. You just throw in a handful of wood shavings after it. Every six months or so you open up the bottom chamber and HEY PRESTO, black odourless soil you shovel out and barrow to your garden.

Not the veggie garden. That would be weird. I guess you could, but we don't . . . yet.

I love having a huge uninterrupted view of the sky, sometimes the moon and the stars feel so close you could grab them. I love being visited by owls, butcher birds and cockatoos. Even the goanna that goes through the bins is part of our circle of friends.

But ultimately it's the people. We have wonderful neighbours, the finest human beings I've ever known. Sure we live here to be around less people but without the people around us life would be a lot harder. And nowhere near as much fun. We love these people, and judging by the amount of help and support we've received over the years, they love us.

Of course a few people in the music press assumed that I'd moved to the country to get away from the vices of the big city and to stay out of reach of the temptation of drug use (even the publisher of this book assumed as much, but he's a dick). Their mistake was to assume there are parts of Australia that are drug free! Maybe there are, but the North Coast of New South Wales ain't one of 'em!

I reckon there are more people per capita up this way who are *on something* than anywhere else in the country. Probably the world. Trust me, it's easier to be stoned or tripping or nodding off when there's warm weather and lots of space around you.

Sure there are drugs around but there's not so much of the 'drug problem' you see on the news. The truth is I know far more functioning drug users up this way than I do in the city.

Take Garry (not his real name) for instance. He's in his sixties, a builder, and a good one. Garry's also the most consistently high human being you'd ever meet. The man drops trips like most people sink beers. This is not a reckless youth hell-bent on irresponsible self-destruction. He knows what he likes and how much to take. He always has a wonderful time and is great company.

That's the real trouble with drugs. PEOPLE! The wrong people are on drugs. It's shitty people that give drugs a bad name. YOU GIVE DRUGS … A BAD NAME. That Bon Jovi song was spot on: Garry on the other hand is a shining example of how to do it (not that I would, good lord no, I don't aspire to be like Garry, but I am in awe).

Some of the people I've met since we've lived here are wilder than any rock'n'roll band I've known. Some of them have a 'been in the jungle too long' vibe, but most are tradies that have bought a bit of land away from the watchful eyes of society to do whatever they want, whenever they want.

And that's the real reason why I moved to the country. To able to go outside and take a piss off my veranda without putting my pants on.

Now look, don't get the wrong idea here. Sure we live in the country, away from the conveniences of life in the big smoke, but we're not exactly 'roughing it'. We're not hippies in a tree house, we have as many mod cons as possible, believe me. Although our internet is shit, so yeah, you wouldn't like it.

EARTH MOTHER SHIELD MAIDENS

Kristyna and I have been together for a long time now and it's been a roller-coaster ride.

At times I've been a dickhead, a fuckwit and an arsehole. But to Kristyna's credit she realised – in fact we both did – that we're a unit, we're a family and we're in it for the long haul. And you don't cut and run when things get shitty and weird, because they won't stay that way forever.

I love her with a depth that couldn't have existed if we hadn't gone through all the sorts of shit we have. Love involves a lot of understanding and forgiveness. If you can't forgive . . . you can't live.

Kristyna is very much her own woman. She's not hanging off me for her identity. She has her own gravity. She's amazing – incredibly down to earth and tough. VERY TOUGH. But also very sensitive and intuitive and VERY FUNNY. Humour is a big part of our life together. We laugh a lot. And our kids laugh a lot. I actually think that is the bottom line and key to happiness in anything – not just relationships.

Kristyna makes me laugh but I don't think I make her laugh that often. She's laughed AT me a fair bit over the years. She's my toughest audience and my harshest critic. She's very supportive but she doesn't fan the flames of my ego – more that she keeps a handle on it with controlled burnings and the occasional bucket of truth. I need that.

But particularly since we moved to the country she's turned into this powerhouse. EVERYTHING that has happened on our property she has done. She's thought of it, sourced the materials, talked to and organised the tradies and seen each project right through.

She has become this amazingly capable, practical person. Anything is possible. It didn't actually seem to develop. It was just suddenly there. It was as though something that had been dormant inside her was accessed in full flight.

One minute she's my rock chick girlfriend, next she's an earth mother-shield maiden.

She knew all about plants, animals, soil types, farming techniques, building materials, alternative medicine and a hundred other things – in fact every single aspect of this life we were entering. And in a pre-Google world. I still don't know how she knows all she knows but she's amazing in the way that she does. Just an incredible human being.

Indeed, truth be told I've been blessed to have been surrounded by strong women all my life. My mother always ran the show in our house when I was growing up.

Tuesday's mum Andrea is another amazing big-hearted woman with a great sense of humour. She's always been and remains an important part of our family. Despite being 'exes' we've made it work and a lot of the credit for that goes to her. She loves and is loved by our other four kids. She's their 'other mother'.

Andrea and Kristyna are good friends. They value each other and they get that we are all working as a team. Lots of people find this hard to believe and over the years the gossipers have run away with all sorts of stories. We just laugh. Believe me, I don't take any of this for granted. I'm so grateful my kids have powerful role models like these women.

For many years that's the way it was: me and Kristyna and the two girls, Tuesday and Scarlet, with the two mums (who all got along well thankfully). Until 2003 . . .

That's when, once again, I heard the words 'I'm late'.

Ede Mae was born in March 2004, and this time I was ready. I knew how to do this thing called fatherhood now, and I actually took the time to enjoy it. We had a good system where Kristyna would deal with the baby's needs during the night and I would take over in the morning while she slept in as long as she needed. That's the good thing about rock'n'roll dads – we may be away sometimes, but when we're there, we're completely there. If I had a nine-to-five job, we couldn't have done it like this.

By now I assumed my lot in life was to be the father of daughters, and I was more than happy with that. But when the family gathered together for Kristyna's ultrasound in early 2010 and the tech said, 'Looks like it's a boy', my jaw hit the floor.

Louie was born in October 2010, and I have to say, that little man has changed my life. I realised that bringing up little girls is like raising angels – beautiful, adorable creatures that you love and protect and look upon with wonder. But ultimately they're like a different species. With Louie I feel an empathy I could never do with the girls, as much as I love them. I'd never felt love for anything or anybody like I had for that boy. Every scratch, every bruise, every laugh and every tear I feel with him, because I've been there myself.

My world was perfect, my heart full.

What more could there be? How about one more?

'Oh okay, why the hell not?' Roy was born in March 2013 and the nice ordered world we'd known tipped over into chaos. Well, not really chaos but let me tell you it was a handful. We'd inadvertently been very clever (none of our pregnancies have been planned) spacing the births of our kids by at least five years so each had time entirely devoted to them.

Never before had I had two of them in nappies at the same time (good God, there was shit everywhere) and a good night's sleep now became a rare and precious thing. But, oh how I love them. My own father never really hugged me and I don't know how he didn't. I hug my kids all the time. Louie knows the value of a good hug, and hugs me right back. Roy struggles and giggles, but he'll learn.

I love many things about parenting, but one thing that's been affirming and reassuring as a musician has been seeing the primal effect of rock'n'roll on my children. I'll never forget the day I was driving with my daughters Scarlet and Tuesday and Deep Purple's 'Smoke on the Water' came on the car stereo. 'Dad . . . what is THIS?' Tuesday inquired breathlessly.

She was ten years old at the time, and I could see that this classic but very basic rock riff had hooked her within seconds.

Louie and Roy love loud rhythmic music. I recently played Public Enemy's *Fear of a Black Planet* on the home stereo and they exploded into all kinds of physical movement.

They love The Sonics, Link Wray, Cypress Hill, Black Sabbath, the Ramones and their favourite Monkees song is 'Steppin' Stone'. Roy is three and really has no frame of reference of how one is supposed to act while listening to rock music, it's pure instinct. Big beats and heavy riffs move my kids just like they do me.

LITTLE ANIMALS

THE BEASTS OF BOURBON / 2007

In late 2005 the band was playing in Europe and Spencer played us a song called 'Thanks' in someone's tiny hotel room after the show one night. Although none of the other songs would sound anything like it, hearing this song made us want to make another album. For some reason we made 'Thanks' the cornerstone of the next record. I guess it's true that an irresponsible dark humour bookends the album.

'Used to give my money to the motherfuckin' poor

But I don't care about nothin' anymore' is the opening line.

We went ahead and recorded this album BEFORE we signed with the legendary Alberts record label so delivered it as is (or as was). It took three days to record and is a credit to all involved but I reckon that's it for this band. Time to move on.

RECORD LABEL: *Albert Music*
CORE BAND MEMBERS: *Tex Perkins (vocals), Spencer P. Jones (guitar), Charlie Owen (guitar), Brian Hooper (bass), Tony Pola (drums).*

ANIMAL FARM

Animals.

Shall we talk about animals? Now, I'm no Dr Dolittle, but I have now had lots of experience with animals since living on the property. Where would you like to start? How about with those majestic creatures known as horses?

Oh yes, we've had horses. Not that long after we move here, the neighbours on the next property told us they were moving out. They had three horses and said, 'We can't take care of these horses, would you take care of them?' We said 'sure', not realising that TAKING CARE of these horses actually meant burying them. They were already pretty old, and one by one over the next few months, they started dropping dead. Burying a horse is a big deal, and has to be done properly or the dead horse will rise from the grave. Literally the corpse swells up like a balloon and if it's not deep enough the ground gradually swells and up she comes.

The last horse was a sweetheart named Jasmine. We got a stallion in to spend some time with her and as a result we got Jasper. Jasmine didn't live for much longer after that so for a long time we just had Jasper, who was a wonderful horse. The sweetest-natured creature I've been lucky enough to ever encounter. A very mellow fellow was our Jasper, but prone to mishaps and injuries. As a result of that we spent a lot of time caring for Jasper's various injuries. I guess I had intended to one day ride him, just because that's what people do, but I never did and I'm glad I didn't turn him into no Beast Of Burden. He was the only horse I ever loved. And then Jasper died. Members of our beautiful community came to comfort him as he passed, struggling for each breath.

One sure thing about owning animals is they will die. You will outlive them. You will see their death. With the horses it was this fucking Crofton weed – it's a very tasty weed and that's the problem. They like it and go for it and then after a year or so, the get fibrosis of the lungs and they die gasping for breath. It's horrible and that's the way that Jasper went. It's a weed that we've tried to eradicate from all the properties up our way but it eventually comes back. It's insidious.

How do you learn about animals? In our case, as you go. We had a heifer die giving birth, but the calf survived. My daughters Tuesday and Ede and a friend of ours, Lilly, hand-reared and bottle-fed Pebbles for months. Lilly would visit us just to come spend time with Pebbles, mothering that cow to a fanatical degree. Now she's full grown she acts just like any other cow – Pebbles not Lilly – but is far more personable than the other cows. That's the key to animal survival: make yourself vulnerable and loveable, and your humans mightn't eat you . . . for a while. No, I'm joking. We would never eat Pebbles, really, trust me.

We had this one bull we called Houdini because he could break out of anything. And mysteriously. We'd get up and he'd be gone and we'd go 'How the hell did he get out of THAT?' There

There's a donkey waiting to see you in the lounge room.

would be no breaks in the fence; he hadn't charged at it. Had he jumped over? Houdini (also known as Black N White and BBQ) would often be found chewing away on grass on the side of the road. People would always complain, saying he was a possible traffic hazard (just slow down, dickhead). Eventually we had to send him off to market. That's not to say he's on someone's plate now. He may have been bought by someone for breeding purposes. He might be in a paddock somewhere with lush green grass and a dozens of heifers to chase around . . . Well, it's possible.

Yes, all those animals have been a handful along the way. But the donkeys. The donkeys are different. The donkeys have a temperament that is just gorgeous. They're the most person-able, curious, gentle, happy animals. And they look forward to interaction with you.

Horses are such big animals and if you're the slightest bit intimidated they feel it and they love it. 'Bit scared are you? – GOOD, I LIKE THAT.' Horses can be intimidating and cows are suspicious and aloof but donkeys are where it's at. When we tell people we have donkeys they will often ask, 'What do you do with them?' As if all animals must have a purpose and a use. What do we do with them? We love them. They make us happy.

So in the donkey world we've had Mr and Mrs Brown, who we got about seven years ago. And then Frieda came along not long after that. She was already pregnant so she had Misty. That left three females for Mr Brown. None of them are technically his offspring so he can have his way with all three – and he has. Mrs Brown has been pregnant again, and so has Frieda, and Misty as well.

So we've had three baby donkeys over the past 18 months. One was born the day Bowie died so we called him Ziggy, and the very latest was born very near to Leonard Cohen's death so he's Lenny. Then there's Eddie . . . I don't know why he's called Eddie. Did Eddie Fisher die last year? Eddie Munster? Eddie McGuire? They're amazing to see immediately after they're born. Minutes after they come out they're up on their feet. After they're all dry and fluffy they are cutest bloody thing you've ever seen.

When it comes to courtship Mr Brown singles out the object of his affection and basically chases her around with this enormous penis, then tries to get into the position. She's just hammering him in the face BANG, BANG, BANG with her back legs that – Jesus Christ – would certainly put me off – but it doesn't deter Mr Brown. It goes on and on until she tires for a few seconds and then IT'S IN. I've never actually seen THE moment but I've certainly seen the long, arduous courtship.

We've also had two dogs over the past 15 years – a border collie and a Jack Russell. Spock and Chella. They were idiot pains in the arse but I loved them, especially the border collie, Spock (Spocky, Spocky Boy, Sporty or anything starting with 'Sp'). But NEEDY. Talk about NEEDY. HEY HEY HEY, HOW ARE YA? HEY HEY HEY? DO YOU LIKE ME? DO YA? HEY HEY HEY, PAT ME, PAT ME. PAT ME. Constantly, desperately in need of affirmation. Needy and annoying and filthy. If there was any cow or horse shit nearby or anything dead or rotting, Spock would find it and roll in it.

Spock was another beautiful soul. I loved that dog with a part of my heart I didn't know existed until he came to us but I must say that now that the dog years are over my life's a lot easier.

Then there was a period when we had no domestic animals around the house.

Spocky Boy.

This was when we spent some more time in Melbourne when Roy was born. While we were away there seemed to be a rat plague generally in the area. Everyone had way more rats around their houses, sheds and properties than they usually did.

So we got back from Melbourne and the place was basically like the Chelsea Hotel for rats. Every possible nook and cranny and space had been inhabited by a rat. Anything that could be chewed, anything that could be destroyed – they were onto it. WHY THE FUCK DO THEY CHEW THROUGH POWER CORDS?

So we had a year-long war with the rats, thinking of ever cleverer ways of killing and catching them. The best one was actually the simplest. We'd done everything – traps, baits, you name it. But the garbage bin half-filled with water, with a bit of PVC pipe fastened to it and stretched across the top of the bin with a bit of bread also fastened to the middle of the pipe, and then you grease the pipe – gets 'em every time. They think THIS LOOKS GOOD – and in they go. We caught half-a-dozen in each bin the first night we did it, but that really didn't make a dent.

They just kept coming until we got BILL THE CAT who is my favourite animal in the world because within two weeks he SORTED THAT SHIT OUT. He'd kill them, chew their heads off and leave their corpses displayed for us for inspection. Strange, but lately he's been eating the rest of the body and leaving the head. Anyway, our life has never been better. Thank you Bill. I love you.

From time to time we have interactions with wild animals as well. Louie is six now but when he was about three months old

I woke up in the middle of the night to the immortal words, 'THERE'S A SNAKE IN THE BED'.

True shit. There was a snake in Louie's bed. It had crawled across our bedhead, past Kristyna's bedside table and down into the crib, which was where half its body was. It was at least five-and-a-half foot long.

Within seconds Kristyna grabbed the baby, handed him to me and told me she was getting something to deal with it. She came back into the room with a broom stick, scooped up the snake, tossed it out into the garden and we were all back asleep again within 10 minutes. Life goes on . . . luckily.

That snake wasn't actually big enough to eat him, but we've seen many dead chickens over the years. The snake kills the chicken and then tries to eat it, realises at some point that it's too big, and coughs it back up . . . whoops.

Occasionally we might see a little baby snake crawling across the deck – they're very docile and easy to pick up and handle. Cutest thing you ever did see. But I leave the big boys alone.

We once watched two large male pythons fighting each other while hanging from the rafters of our shed. And then observed the incredible harmonious entwining later that night of the victor and his new mating female. Or maybe they were females fighting over a male, I dunno. As I said, I leave the big boys and girls alone.

There is one we see on the driveway occasionally. Snakes like lying on roads at night because they hold the heat for a while. This one, from head-to-tail, stretches all the way across. It's longer than the width of the driveway, which is three metres – that's a 10-foot long snake! And believe me, you can't just drive over it. Apart from being a really shitty thing to do, you'd have trouble getting over! It's THICK. So you have to, very gently, encourage it to move along . . . without pissing it off.

We have a fair number of snakes around the property and traditionally that's always good. But when we had the plague of rats the pythons only picked off one or two. They were no good at truly keeping the numbers down. Not like Bill is. They were just exploiting the situation. They never wanted it to end. Come to think of it now we have cats and therefore less rats we see less snakes . . . so there is a downside to it.

The episode with Louie in the crib was the creepiest thing that's happened but generally we don't mind pythons being around. They're not dangerous snakes – unless they think they can eat you.

WHERE THERE'S SMOKE

THE CRUEL SEA / 2001

Just about my favourite Cruel Sea album recorded with
Magoo at Rocking Horse studios in the hills of the shire
of Byron. All the things we'd been trying to do on the last
record happened a lot easier and more convincingly with
a reunited, relatively clean band and just one focused
producer. It had a good heart; loose but tight enough to be
funky, and a mischievous approach to the production made
our use of samples a lot more fun than on the last record.
This time we used them because we wanted to; last time we
used them because we HAD to.

RECORD LABEL: *Universal*
CORE BAND MEMBERS: *Tex Perkins (vocals), Danny Rumour (guitar),
Jim Elliot (drums), Ken Gormley (bass), James Cruikshank (keyboards/guitar).*

HARBINGERS OF THE APOCALYPSE

The launch for The Cruel Sea's *Where There's Smoke* was on 11 September 2001 at a venue called The Laundry in Melbourne.

After the gig we were back at our hotel and Kenny rings my room and says, 'Just turn on the TV.' Live coverage on every channel, the World Trade Center in New York. I saw the second plane hit. I saw the frickin' things collapse right there in front of me, neat and quick, like the fucking Dean brothers used to demolish buildings in the middle of the night in Queensland in the '70s and '80s. Then another building falls that wasn't even hit. What the fuck? Then they say another has hit the Pentagon. Wow, these terror dudes are good, it's almost as if they had help. But apparently that's crazy talk.

The next day we played Geelong as the start of this massive national tour and there was hardly anyone there. I wasn't surprised. Everyone was still in shock.

After this all our songs took on a different context. 'Jet planes fly tooo high' suddenly seemed loaded with new meaning and *Where There's Smoke* – the name of the tour and album for fuck's sake – bordered on sacrilegious. Every time you saw a newspaper or TV you saw plumes of smoke. Mountains of smoke. Smoke smoke SMOKE. Was the fact The Cruel Sea travelled under this banner simply incredibly bad timing or could it be seen as incredibly insensitive? Maybe no one even noticed.

I mean it was way too soon for any attitude but shock and fear at this point. Or was it providence? Had we inadvertently become the harbingers of Armageddon. Armageddon outta here! And believe me, people WERE very sensitive to all this at the time. The rock band Shihad announced that they were changing their name to Pacifier because Shihad sounded too much like jihad. And then the rock band Frenzal Rhomb announced they were changing their name to Shihad. Hilarious.

After that first dud gig in Geelong, the tour went well and we had huge crowds. Huge crowds full of people who seemed to have the attitude that this might be their last chance. Last chance to dance, last chance to get wasted, last chance for love. There was an abandon that translated into, WE MIGHT BE DEAD IN A WEEK, LET'S GET IT ON.

No one really knew how America was going to respond and there was a real feeling that now that this had happened, anything was possible! If they can do that, they can get you anywhere. All the world's a potential battlefield now.

Was there going to be a war? You bet! That would involve nuclear weapons? Maybe. I felt it too. Now everything I saw, I saw in that context. Every gig was like a farewell show. Being on tour can get kinda otherworldly, with all the travelling and drinking, and so with this atmosphere, one's behaviour takes on a rarefied air.

'Nothing matters anymore' became the unofficial theme for the tour, even though suddenly flying turned into a very serious business. Stringent airport security became the new norm. ID checks, bag checks, body checks, shoe checks and arse checks. It felt like the world had changed and no one knew what was going to happen. Paranoia was everywhere, but I floated through it, either drunk, stoned or hungover.

Numb, untouched.

I just needed to get home before the whole thing blew.

Looking back, things didn't explode or implode with The Cruel Sea. They just slowly wound down. As time went by between gigs, the fact that we hadn't played for long periods wasn't really as big an issue to us as other people seemed to assume it was. Sometimes we would just give it a rest – I would go work with someone else for a while and there was never a specific time period determined about when we'd get back together. As far as I was concerned it could be months – or years – but I'd always come back to The Cruel Sea.

That's been a thing with a lot of my bands: there's no real need to break up or make some formal announcement and all that bullshit. You just walk away from it and maybe you walk back and maybe you don't. There's no THIS IS THE END press release.

I was often asked why The Cruel Sea ended – but the thing is that as far as I was concerned we hadn't ended. We always planned to do another Cruel Sea record – we just didn't know when. There was never a time when it was 'WE WILL NEVER EVER PLAY AGAIN.'

But then James died.

We *will* never play again now that Cruickers is gone. It's still hard for me to get my head around the idea that I'll never see him again. James had been a constant in my life for so long, and we'd had so many adventures, sometimes I forget he's gone and briefly think about discussing a movie or a book with him, and then I remember.

Of course The Cruel Sea existed before James but there was such a long period of time when it was the five of us. James was an important part of it and if in the very unlikely circumstances that the rest of us did play together again it would be something very, very different.

But I wouldn't hold my breath.

LADYBOYZ

When Lou Reed released *Metal Machine Music* in 1975 it was widely considered to be a begrudging contractual fulfilment.

A 'fuck you I'm outta here' to RCA, his record company. 'Music' SO extreme it was deemed unlistenable, and therefore unsaleable. Rock critics hated it. 'The spin cycle of a washing machine has more melodic variation than *Metal Machine Music*,' said one unamused pants wetter. Lou lost fans and credibility within the straight rock world. I gotta admit, I've never got all the way through it, and I'm a noise lover.

When the Rolling Stones, at the end of their contract with DECCA Records, were told they were contracted for one more single, they gave them 'Cocksucker Blues'.

My favourite Monty Python record is the *Contractual Obligation Album*. A supposed grab bag of throwaway songs and skits.

So I was very familiar with this concept by the time the dweeb at Universal suggested I record an album of covers.

After the sneer dropped from my face, I said, 'Sure, as long as it counts as my final contracted album.'

I'll give them a fucking covers album, I thought.

And not only did they suggest a covers album but that – and this is a great example of record company creativity – it should feature . . . CELEBRITY GUESTS.

From this came the Ladyboyz – or to give the band its full and correct title – Tex Perkins & His Ladyboyz. Doing covers was already a well-established tradition with lots of bands I was involved with, in that when we did cover versions we'd do ironic versions of songs that we really didn't like. But to record an album of that crap, on a major record label? It was like our very own *Great Rock'n'Roll Swindle*.

I'd done this sort of thing before with a band called Hot Property, which was basically a forerunner of the Ladyboyz. Both bands did versions of shit songs from the '70s and '80s (and this was IN the '80s). Hot Property was a very danger-ous band to be in. Seriously. In Sydney we would play our regular haunts, mostly to people who were in on the joke. But when we played Melbourne supporting The Johnnys, we played to people who had no idea what we were doing. We collided with people that did not get it. They hated us! To an hilarious degree. We played Chasers Nightclub (yes it's been there that long) and this guy walks up onto the stage and spits in my face in disgust. Then, wearing platform shoes and a red flared pants suit (known as 'The Red Gear'), I launched myself onto his back as he re-entered the crowd, crashing to the floor.

We played the Village Green hotel way out in the suburbs and had to have security escort us off the premises. People wanted to hurt us. People were asking for their money back, and we were just the support band!

So I was familiar with pissing people off in that way.

Anyway I made sure the album we did would count as a contractual tick in the contractual box as usually covers albums aren't considered 'proper' albums when you're contracted to give a record company a certain number of albums. But I made sure they agreed that this would be considered a real album and would count as the album I needed to deliver to conclude my obligations to them. Then I would be FREE!

I decided that this project should be best described as 'experimental cabaret music'. It was my version of what Lou Reed did with *Metal Machine Music*, except that his record company hadn't asked for that as the final album in his contract. My record company *had* asked for this. Oh yes, they said they wanted a covers album. I gave them a covers album.

I needed some accomplices in this pop crime. A project like this deserved the best players in the world. Slash, Steve Stevens and Skunk Baxter were among the many I couldn't afford. So instead I enlisted James Cruickshank, Charlie Owen, Joel Silbersher, Pat Bourke and Gus Agars. Meet the Ladyboyz.

Let's not forget, the label had requested celebrity guests. So I gave them celebrity guests. I gave them damn good celebrity guests too. Jimmy Barnes was up for it so he sang on our version of The Stylistics' song 'You Make Me Feel Brand New'. Nic Chester from Jet is on 'Hold The Line' by Toto. Suze DeMarchi does her bit on Bob Seger's 'We've Got Tonight' and Adalita Srsen was totally in to singing Alice Cooper's 'You And Me'.

Are you getting the picture here? We did songs like Dr Hook's creepy classic 'Love You A Little Bit More', Mondo Rock's even creepier classic, 'Come Said The Boy', Hall & Oates' 'Rich Girl' and Nik Kershaw's 'Wouldn't It Be Good' and so on.

If I suggested a song to the band and they said, 'Oh no, not that!' it was in! Some people – not many, mind you – totally love the record, but more people than that have never forgiven me for it. We called the album *No. 1'S & No. 2'S*.

The tour to promote the Ladyboyz album involved us playing casinos. The idea there was to play the tackiest places we could find to play – and those places were usually casinos.

In keeping with current merchandising trends, we also developed our own fragrance, Scent of a Lady Boy. We did the Palms at the Crown Casino in Melbourne and that was actually spectacular. Everyone there got the joke and were working with us on it.

But at other places it wasn't quite the same and people were baffled. We played the Country Club Casino in Launceston in Tasmania. After the show the backstage door bursts open and this woman stands in the doorway and screams at us – 'YOU SHOULD BE ASHAMED OF YOURSELVES! YOU CALL YOURSELVES THE FIFTH BEST COVERS BAND IN THE COUNTRY. YOU'RE NOT!'

That came about because the press release, obviously written as a bit of a joke, described us as 'arguably the fifth best covers band in Australia'. This was repeated around the country in stories by cut-and-paste journalists writing newspaper articles, pretty much as we expected it to be and without any sense of irony. But hey, it says 'arguably'.

This woman thought it would be good to see the fifth best covers band in the country and she was very disappointed. In fact, she was furious. One of our crew, Henry, tried to close the door to keep her out but she's pushing back. Screaming and beating on the door as it closes. 'YOU'RE A DISGRACE.' All the band aghast at the onslaught of passionate abuse.

Well done, gentlemen!

We played Star City in Sydney, Wrest Point in Hobart and Twin Towns on the Gold Coast. We stayed within the conceptual framework of playing horrible music in horrible places. The critics were divided in their response to the album. Some happy to run with the gag, others vowing never to listen to another Tex Perkins record as long as they live. Hilarious.

But even though the album and tour was delivered to the record company as a kind of middle-finger thing we enjoyed the hell out of it, and it's a lot more fun to listen to than *Metal Machine Music.*

NO. 1'S &
NO. 2'S

TEX PERKINS & HIS LADYBOYZ /
2008

Tim Spicer was the one responsible for helping us commit
this crime against my career. This could've been called
Career Suicide Attempt. Covers of classic soft rock hits
of the '70s and '80s polarised the critics and the public
alike. But really, it's all about the infomercial. Instead of
using the video budget to make music videos we made
an infomercial. We even bought some time on late-night
telly and ran it like it was real, which it was – sort of.
The album's okay but the infomercial is really where the
project peaked. But you gotta have an album if you wanna
have an infomercial, I suppose.

RECORD LABEL: *Universal*
CORE BAND MEMBERS: *Tex Perkins (vocals), James Cruikshank (piano),
Charlie Owen (guitar), Joe Silbersher (guitar), Patrick Bourke (bass),
Gus Agars (drums).*

THE DARK HORSES

I met Murray Paterson sometime in 1998.

Our good friend Justine Clarke was visiting the area and was bringing with her her new boyfriend, Murray.

I liked Murray straightaway. He was good-humoured, worldly, open-hearted and as it turned out, a great guitar player. He's a Doctor of Philosophy, which meant he was giving lectures on Art at Southern Cross University. Murray, with his flaming red hair, is also a great surfer, possessing an uncanny ability to read the surf and pick the right wave, not wasting any energy on duds.

The first 'recognition of a kindred spirit' we had was when he spotted the Van Morrison album *Veedon Fleece* in my CD collection. Both of us have a deep connection to this incredible record and we still treat the playing of this record as an almost sacred moment.

We started writing songs soon after we met. Murray had an openness that made writing easy and enjoyable. A lot of people I'd tried to write with over the years had been too cautious and guarded. Frightened of exposing themselves. Writing in that atmosphere can be like pulling teeth. Murray wasn't like that at all, and it was easy to get swept along with his enthusiasm. It also helped that the things he had to offer were really good and unlike anybody else I'd worked with. A beautiful finger-picking style that made standard chords sound unique. No one plays a B minor like Murray Paterson. We wrote two songs, 'Ice In The Sun' and 'Fine Mess' very early on in our partnership. Around the same time, I had written a few by myself, and was amassing a bunch of songs to record for my, by now overdue, second solo album.

I had decided to go back to my old team of Charlie Owen and Tony Cohen to help me bring the album together. Charlie and I hadn't written anything together for a while but he seemed like the right person for me to work with. When we started recording the album, it was just the three of us. I would sing and play guitar, Charlie

Charlie and me at the Hopetoun hotel, 2003.

would do whatever else was necessary and Tony would record it. Charlie can and did play drums, bass, piano, banjo and of course guitars.

A fourth important individual that came into the mix at this stage was Joel.

Joel Silbersher is another unique specimen. A very funny and talented fellow, he was in a band called GOD when he was 15. They had a kind of a hit with a song called 'My Pal'. I had met Joel because he and Charlie had formed a group they called Tendrils. Joel was and still is a great player and he and I wrote a couple of songs together for the album. Joel brought a dark sense of humour and a deep cynicism about . . . everything. It was hard to get a positive word out of Joel so when he said he liked something we did, I knew we'd really got somewhere.

I guess Joel's suspicion and reluctance was a good counter-balance to Murray's enthusiasm.

We used drum loops for a lot of the songs but for one or two our old friend Jim White was kind enough to share his extra-ordinary skinsmanship with us.

These recordings became the album *Dark Horses*. So when the time came to promote the record and play live, I called the band The Dark Horses. Murray fit in very well with his Horse colleagues and they've all become lifelong friends. The core of the band has stayed the same since then.

Murray and Justine stopped seeing each other, but I kept seeing Murray. It took a long time for Murray to get over his breakup with Justine – so many heartbroken, melancholic melodies sprang from his hands and inhabit a lot of our collaborations.

Over the years I've started doing a lot of shows with just Murray and me. I've also done shows with just Charlie. But these days it's usually me and Murray.

Doing those duo shows is an economical thing as much as anything. With The Dark Horses there's six people plus a front-of-house guy and a stage guy. You're dragging around at least eight people, so over the years there's been more and more of these stripped-back gigs.

Murray and I just have this easy relationship doing the shows together. We don't actually hang out that much up north. It's hard to get him out of the house these days. But if one of us has something, we'll find the time.

In the early days we'd record ideas onto a cassette into a ghetto blaster and swap tapes, and then CDs. Now it's MP3s so the relationship has spanned a few different technologies.

When it comes to songwriting I still don't have a formula of any kind. The whole thing is still a mystery to me. I plan to keep it that way for as long as possible.

I recently wrote a song called 'A Man In Conflict With Nature'. Murray had given me a rough recording of him playing and sort of mumbling a few words here and there. For some reason the word DOGS stuck out as I listened through this shadowy folk tune. I had my first line.

'WENT DOWN TO THE DOGS . . . ON SATURDAY NIGHT.' As soon as I had that, the rest of it rolled out very easily. Mind you I didn't actually write anything down. I had the song on recording function on my computer, so whenever I thought of a line I sang it straight into the song. No paper.

Murray Paterson yelling the chords
in my ear during a show in 2015.

Some of the songs we write together find homes in other projects that I do, especially things like Tex, Don & Charlie. 'Whenever It Snows', 'Paycheques' and 'Someday I'll Forget' are all Paterson–Perkins co-writes. On the new Tex, Don & Charlie album I have five songs – three written with Murray.

Murray has a very certain style of writing that leads me down Melancholy Street a lot of the time. The words I hear within his music are world weary, sometimes lost, sometimes broken. But always with a strength and beauty. When Rachel Ward asked me to provide the music for her film *Beautiful Kate*, Murray was the first and only person I thought of to work with.

I have never been, and never will be a great guitar player, but I will persist. Trouble is, to be really good, you've got to love the thing. And Mo LOVES his guitar, a 1961 baby Martin. He cares for it like the special instrument it is. I've stopped out and out abuse of my instruments, but I'll never get to that stage. As I sit here writing this, I don't even know where my guitars are. All three of them. Murray would never NOT know where his guitar is, not for a second. But maybe that's part of our schtick – we're the Odd Couple of guitar interplay.

Usually it's me bashing out chords and him putting something nice and pretty over the top of it. Or it might be him doing some nice chords and me playing very basic lead. Murray brings a quality that I can't achieve by myself. For starters he can actually play.

Charlie Owen, Joel Silbersher and Murray Paterson: I hope I am able to make music in some form with all of these frisky little ponies for many years to come.

The Dark Horses may continue as a band, and it may not. Maybe we'll just change names.

Just to keep things confusing.

DARK HORSES

TEX PERKINS / 2000

This album I demoed at home on 4-track and then
presented the songs to Charlie Owen and Tony Cohen.
We started the album with just the three of us. I sang
and played guitar and Charlie played whatever else was
necessary. It took about a week using drum loops and
guest musicians, and includes two co-writes with Murray
Paterson, two with Joel Silbersher and one with Rowland
S. Howard, I think this one sits somewhere in my top 10
albums by me. 'She Speaks A Different Language' and
'Ice In The Sun' are two of my favourite songs that I've
written, but we learned out on the road how much songs
like 'Please Break Me Gently' and 'To Us' meant to people.

RECORD LABEL: *Grudge*
CORE BAND MEMBERS: *Tex Perkins (vocals/guitar), Charlie Owen (guitar/piano/
keyboards), Jim White (drums), Murray Paterson (guitar), Joel Silbersher
(bass/guitar).*

SWEET NOTHING

TEX PERKINS' DARK HORSES / 2003

Recorded at my old place with Jeff Lovejoy and a mobile recording studio, which is basically the desk and all the outboard gear that you'd normally have in a recording studio except it's in road cases so they could be transported to wherever you liked. Wherever we liked was my old house in the country.

Once again, some good things here but all in all, not a great record.

RECORD LABEL: *Universal*
CORE BAND MEMBERS: *Tex Perkins (vocals/guitar), Charlie Owen (guitar/piano/keyboards/synth), Murray Paterson (guitar), Joel Silbersher (bass), Scritch (drums).*

BEAUTIFUL KATE

FILM SOUNDTRACK

TEX PERKINS AND MURRAY PATERSON / 2008

Rachel Ward asked me to write and record the music for her first film as director. Murray was the first person I thought of to help me. A lot of this music is our two acoustic guitars. The theme to the movie was written before we even read the script. We recorded a couple of things and sent them to Rachel just to see if we were on the right track. 'It's perfect', was her response. The first piece we sent became the main theme. 'This is going to be easy', we thought. Well, it was, and it wasn't. Some things we wrote and we left it up to the filmmakers to decide where to put it, but other times they were ultra-specific, asking for pieces of music of specific length that did certain things and hit various emotional points in specific places. It was a great challenge and a great pleasure. This one's up there for me.

RECORD LABEL: *Level Two Music*
CORE BAND MEMBERS: *Tex Perkins (vocals/guitar), Murray Paterson (guitar), Kristyna Higgins (slide guitar).*

TEX PERKINS & THE DARK HORSES

TEX PERKINS & THE DARK
HORSES / 2010

Recorded at Magoo's church studio Applewood, we brought
a stockpile of songs that had accumulated over the last
few years, and it was time to record them. Mostly songs
I'd co-written with Murray, there's some good stuff here.
Because there had been a drought we thought it best to try
to record as many songs as possible, aiming for a double
album. But what we ended up with was an overcrowded
single album. I like this album but it's another example of
'would've been a better record with less songs'.

RECORD LABEL: *Inertia Music*
CORE BAND MEMBERS: *Tex Perkins (vocals/guitar), Charlie Owen (guitar/piano/
keyboards/synth), Jim White (drums), Joel Silbersher (bass/guitar),
Gus Agars (drums), Steve Hadley (bass).*

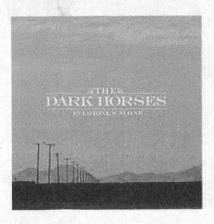

EVERYONE'S ALONE

TEX PERKINS & THE DARK HORSES / 2012

After waiting seven years between *Sweet Nothing* and the last album, I wanted to see what it would be like to make the next album much sooner rather than later, while the band was still 'warm'. We did a five-day session with Roger Bergodaz at the end of the tour for our previous album and threw what we had at each other. This made for unusual contributions. Most of the album has a stripped-back futuristic, hungover, country-folk feel as slide guitars meet synthesisers, but occasionally an aberration like Joel's 'A Real Job' pops up and radically changes the mood. This album is also the last time we would record with James Cruickshank as he left for Berlin soon after. When he returned he was too ill to play and died a year later in 2015. Now that he's gone, recordings of James's vocals, keyboards and guitar seem to stand out – my ear going towards his parts more than the other components of the song.

RECORD LABEL: *Inertia Music*
CORE BAND MEMBERS: *Tex Perkins (vocals/guitar), Murray Paterson (guitar), Charlie Owen (guitar/piano/keyboards/synth), Joel Silbersher (guitar/bass), Steve Hadley (bass), Gus Agars (drums), James Cruickshank (piano).*

TUNNEL AT THE END OF THE LIGHT

TEX PERKINS & THE DARK HORSES / 2015

Another quick one with Roger Bergodaz, this one completes the trio of Dark Horses albums we made since 2010. I think the track 'Slide On By' is our most successful attempt here. Built around an irresistible riff from Joel we let this epic unravel over eight minutes of atmospheric groove. Other things like the ghostly melodies of Murray's instrumental 'The View South' are given plenty of space to drift like currents in a river. Thematically it's an outward-looking record but occasionally it is extremely intimate. 'All Is Quiet' explores a magical night of resignation to insomnia.

RECORD LABEL: *Inertia Music*
CORE BAND MEMBERS: *Tex Perkins (vocals/guitar/harmonica), Murray Paterson (guitar), Charlie Owen (guitar/piano/keyboards/synth), Joel Silbersher (guitar/bass), Steve Hadley (bass), Gus Agars (drums).*

HELLO, I'm JOHNNY CASH

I'd never really imagined I'd be in a theatre show and working as an actor of sorts and doing a musical show based around the life of Johnny Cash.

I didn't see that one coming – but it actually came into my life at pretty much the right time. Certainly the most convenient time. It came along at exactly the time when I didn't want to make a record.

Let me explain. The Ladyboyz album came out in 2008 and effectively I'd then completed and delivered everything I was signed up to do. That was the good part. The not so good part was the clause in the contract saying that everything I did in the 12-month period after the contract ended – they had their claws into that if they wanted. This meant that whatever I recorded in the next year I had to play to Universal and then they could decide whether or not they wanted to release it.

So armed with that knowledge it was pretty easy to work out what the Tex position on this was going to be. I'M NOT GOING TO MAKE A RECORD FOR THE NEXT YEAR was the no-brainer decision.

Then, out of the blue I had an approach from 'The Theatre World', asking whether I was interested in doing a show based on the life of Johnny Cash.

Their idea was that rather than get someone from 'The Theatre World' they'd get someone from 'The Rock'n'Roll World' with some sort of 'reputation'. They also said that they needed this 'Rock'n'Roll Person' to have a checkered career and a tenor voice. Guess who?

Strangely, they had no idea about my pre-existing fondness for Johnny Cash or that The Dum Dums had played a lot of Cash's songs.

But in the end it was absolutely perfect for me. Too perfect. I figured this would be a good way to kill a few months doing something that came easily to me, ticking off the time on that 12 months I was beholden to Universal, and then I'd go back to my usual stuff. And also it was a bit of a career change because even though I fit very easily and comfortably into the Johnny Cash thing, this was something I'd never done before. It was a challenge to learn about and get experience in the theatre and doing this style of musical-meets-narrative performance.

Then the show just took off. I had no idea at the time that almost 10 years later I'd still be touring around the country doing Johnny fucking Cash shows.

THE MAN IN BLACK

So, suddenly I'm working on this show about the life of Johnny Cash.

The script for the production was written and owned – if owned is the right word here – by this guy from the 'theatre world' called Jim McPherson. It's his thing. He 'created' it.

The original script that was presented to me was the one he'd written. This is the first time I think they were surprised to realise that this rock guy actually knew a bit about Johnny Cash. I pointed out to them that the script ended just like the movie did, in 1968 after he successfully did the show at Folsom Prison.

The script then just ignores everything that happened after that – which if my maths is correct is about four decades. It's a bit like doing a show on Bob Dylan and stopping after he had his alleged motorbike accident in Woodstock in 1969.

Okay, I'll concede that there was a lot of Cash stuff in the 1980s that is pretty easy to ignore, but he was still out there making music even if he wasn't that fashionable and that to me is an interesting story in itself. But it also ignored the whole American Recordings period, all those amazing albums he did with Rick Rubin from 1994 onwards. The writer and producers were completely unaware that this stuff existed. So I had to explain that there was a really great period of music there that's almost the equal of his early work.

They were a bit taken aback by this, and the fact that I was actually informing them about huge slabs of the Johnny Cash story – but they really should have known more about him if they were seriously going to do a show about him. So we just got stuck into the script. Cutting out chunks of flabby dialogue and rewriting much of it. I put in songs that maybe some other people wouldn't have. Obviously there's songs you have to do if you're doing a Johnny Cash show but I certainly steered it in a direction that was more to my liking.

The script is essentially based around the song selection which serves the narrative. We weaved dialogue in and around the songs. As it went on we slowly whittled the original outline down to the show that it ultimately became. I'd throw in gags here and there to lighten it up when I thought it needed it.

In the early days of the show the band was the RocKwiz guys. So Pete Luscombe on drums, James Black and Ash Naylor on guitars, and Steve Hadley on double bass. Those guys were the Tennessee Four and so that was really, really good band right there. They worked with us through the construction of the show and did the first season at the Athenaeum Theatre in 2009 and I give them a lot of credit for getting it to where we needed it to be. But after that the B team of Dave Folley, Shane Riley and Matt Walker became the A Team, and have been with the show ever since.

We had Rachel Tidd playing June and she carries most of the real serious weight of the show. I do more the vibes and anecdotal stuff, and she's more the nuts and bolts, which is important in a show like this and in making it work as well as it does. She's the newsreader, the straight person, who delivers all the dry facts that have to be in there – and then I throw in the 'and then Johnny fucked up' bits. So I sort of get it easy in that department.

Backstage before a Man in Black show with Rachel Tidd.

The show was intended to be reverential but also have a tongue-in-cheek side to it, and I think it works in that way. It's a show after all and people want to be entertained. It's almost like a music-driven spoken-word documentary.

I don't try to totally be Johnny Cash – anytime I had to quote him, sure, I'd do an impression of his voice but without overdoing it. I wanted the audience to feel like it was being delivered directly from Cash's perspective, but I also wanted to make sure they didn't feel like they were sitting in class getting a history lesson.

Of course it's a fine line of keeping that balance between being Tex Perkins and then Tex Perkins being Johnny Cash. There's times I'll just use my own voice and other times I definitely sound more like him. Certainly there's big parts of the show when I inhabit him. Doing a show like this is a bit like the way Cash sings a song like 'A Boy Named Sue'. Essentially it's a cover version because the song was written by Shel Silverstein, but the way he sings it, he totally owns it and it's his song. You can't imagine anyone else singing it.

The show does what it has to in order to be a Johnny Cash show – it goes back to the Sun Records stuff and there's a lot from that era as they're the songs that most people know. And there's a lot of the prison stuff as well. But then we include a version of 'Hurt', the song written by Nine Inch Nails that he covered on one of the American Recordings albums. It's a great song – his cover eclipses the original. So when it gets to me, I'm doing a cover of a cover. Likewise, his version of Nick Lowe's 'The Beast In Me' is also great for the narrative.

I managed to persuade the producers to include other things that I love that most people don't know. I love his version of the song 'Bad News' which is just plain weird and unlike anything else he ever recorded.

I don't think anyone expected the show to be as popular as it was. It just kept rolling on and getting bigger and bigger. We did a couple of weeks at the Athenaeum which was the initial season. That was something like 12 shows in a row and I remember thinking to myself, 'How am I going to keep THIS up?' Then they booked SEVEN WEEKS at the Twelfth Night Theatre in Brisbane. They just kept adding shows. In Brisbane we had Monday off but we'd do two shows on a Sunday or Saturday so it was still seven shows a week. I have to admit I went a little insane. Doing a show about someone who was out of it a lot gave me the right to BE out of it a lot. If I stumbled or messed up in any way, it just looked like I was 'being Johnny'. (Hey Joaquin Phoenix, I'm still here too!) In the end we did hundreds of shows right around the country.

Can you imagine?

Doing Brisbane at that stage was good because of course my family came – and it was nice that I was in a show that wasn't loud, in-your-face rock'n' roll with people yelling abuse at me. They could come and see it and be comfortable and have a seat, instead of standing tentatively in a sweaty pub or dingy nightclub.

The previous time my mother had come to see me perform it was with the Beasts. That was a mistake, as the abuse I copped from the Brisbane pieces of shit was astounding. Everything was directed towards me and there was a lot of abuse – 'WANKER!' – and my mother was in the audience. In other circumstances I'd be giving it back to the crowd but on this night I didn't say a word. I held my tongue and hoped her earplugs were thick ones.

When I was starting to do all this there was absolutely no encouragement from my family, not that I needed it. But it's the usual thing – as soon as I was achieving some kind success it was all ownership. That's our boy. But that's fine. My relationship with my mother has always been great and still is. I love my mum, full stop. Simple as that. She's 86 now. There was at least 10 years of, 'Oh, Greg', but then she saw me on television once with The Cruel Sea in the early '90s and suddenly the refrain changed to, 'That's my son!'

When my mother did finally embrace the idea that her son was in show business there was an ABC radio show in Brisbane that she used to listen to. She was listening one day and someone called in and mentioned The Cruel Sea and the radio host uttered the immortal words, 'Who's The Cruel Sea?' Well, my mother got on the phone and set him straight. She couldn't help herself. She had to fill him in on who Tex Perkins was and who The Cruel Sea were and all their wonderful achievements.

Anyway, the radio show's producer kept her number and whenever there was a quiet moment on his show the host would go, 'Well, I might give Mrs Perkins a call and see what she's up to.' This went on for years.

Before you ask, my parents really never called me Tex. It was either 'Greg' or 'darling'. At some stage I was aware of my dad referring to me as Tex to other people but he didn't address me directly that way. When he was talking to other people it was simpler for him to use Tex so people knew who he was talking about.

Now here I am performing as Johnny Cash maybe 15 years since that Beasts Of Bourbon show where I copped all that abuse, so it's really nice for them to be able to come to this. And for Dad to be there this time too. They came – as parents do – to the Sunday matinee. In fact, they came five times and it brought the old fella to tears.

Dad wasn't a Johnny Cash fan per se, the music he related to came from before World War II. He had that album of Marty Robbins *Gunfighter Ballads and Trail Songs*, although I suspect that was because Mum had joined one of those record clubs where when you signed up you got 10 records for ten dollars and she'd told Dad to pick one and he'd seen *Gunfighter Ballads* and pointed at it in the catalogue. But he did like the record and Johnny Cash isn't too far from that.

When I came in to 'The Theatre World' I realised it was very different from what I'd done before. There were people for EVERY job – and it seemed to me there were people employed for jobs that didn't exist, or certainly jobs that didn't require multiple people to do them. There was a lighting designer, a lighting operator AND a lighting director. Really?

But slowly people would get screwed and not get paid and then they'd disappear from the crew and we'd hear all these rumours of disgruntlement. It was like the producers and crew were having their own cannibal war.

I'd come in at the beginning and basically made the show what it was but of course I didn't have ownership of it. Eventually it was just me, Rachel, the band and the front-of-house guy and a stage tech. We'd go into theatres for a season and aside from the existing staff at the theatre it was just us. We'd gone from this crazily over-populated world to virtually no one.

As things progressed the relationship with management became distant. As the show went on, we didn't see the producers that much anymore. It really became *our* show and we refined and changed it whenever we felt it necessary.

Then I decided to take a break from it.

A year or two later the Sydney Festival popped up and asked if I'd like to use Parramatta Jail as the venue for a Johnny Cash-prison style show. They thought it was a great idea if we did a Cash show there. They called it *Far From Folsom*. And it's expanded from those shows to be one that I do in old prisons right around the country.

This show takes the Folsom Prison shows as a context. It's like we try to imagine what would happen if Johnny Cash came and played at whatever prison it is. That allows us a little more freedom as we're not recreating a specific show, we're using it more as a template. It's more about creating the vibe of what a Johnny Cash show in a prison might have been like. And at those gigs he played a certain kind of show – the outlaw songs, the strange funny songs, the more fucked-up stuff and less of the romantic and religious ones.

People love coming inside an old jail and seeing entertainment that is conceptually linked to that location. It's pretty irresistible. To go into these places and learn of the stories, myths and legends of all these incredible locations is really interesting to me. We even played Port Arthur. Like Johnny's original shows, performing there was almost like a kind of cleansing. Bringing a fresh spirit to a place usually associated with misery and tragedy.

Of course some people think any kind of tribute show is uncool and being involved in one compromises one's credibility. Fuck 'em. At the end of the day, this is entertainment, I'm an entertainer, and I'm only too happy to enter-fucking-tain you.

I still do all these other things but I'm very grateful to be able to sing some Cash and make a little at the same time.

My other, other family, I love these people: Shane Riley, Rachel Tidd, Perko, Dave Foley, Steve Hadley and Matt Walker.

TEX PERKINS & THE BAND OF GOLD

TEX PERKINS & THE BAND
OF GOLD / 2010

This album grew out of a hundred sound checks during
The Man In Black run of shows. For our own enjoyment,
we would learn and record an old country tune (anything
that wasn't Johnny Cash) each sound check. Rachel
Tidd is so great to sing with so we chose songs that lent
themselves to a verse-swapping duet style. Steve Hadley
wasted no time getting us into a recording studio. Songs
by Guy Clarke, Townes Van Zandt, Kris Kristofferson and
Porter Wagner were a joy to sing and before we knew it we
had an album.

RECORD LABEL: *Inertia Music*
CORE BAND MEMBERS: *Tex Perkins (vocals), Rachel Tidd (vocals),
Shane Reilly (guitars), Shannon Bourke (guitar), Steve Hadley (bass),
Dave Foley (drums).*

T'N'T

T and I got first and second prize in the international pouting championships 2006.

Us rock guys are a funny lot.

We're very supportive of each other a lot of the time and sincerely wish each other well. But deep down a simmering jealousy takes hold if one of us 'does well'. We just can't help it.

I've known Tim Rogers for a long time and as much as we were, and are, great friends, we have always been, and still are, rivals. I think that's the dynamic and it works fine as we both understand that this is the situation. Both of us would like a little of what we think the other has and they don't . . . whatever that is.

Tim's a naturally competitive person rather than a collaborative person. When we started working together he hadn't really written with other people before. He was very much a 'this is MY baby' kind of guy. Which is fair enough – he's that good.

So when we got together to do the T'n'T project, that was the first time he really allowed himself to do any sort of sharing of a creative platform. I know You Am I songs are delivered fully formed to the other guys in the band.

The T'n'T (that's Tim'n'Tex in case you haven't cottoned on yet) album just grew out of the fact that we were spending time together. Sometime in early 2005 I was asked by Andy Kent of You Am I to guest vocal at an APRA awards or ARIA or something as they were inducting The Easybeats into the Hall Of Fame. I could sing any number of tunes, I chose 'St Louis'.

The rumour mill, the grapevine and gossip columns were overloaded at the time with talk of a series of meltdowns from Tim, the most notorious involving Missy Higgins and a staircase. When I met the band for rehearsals the night before, Tim was in good form and the band sounded great but when we finished, it was on!

We reconvened at the hotel bar where everyone involved in the awards was staying. Tim was amazing, spreading his drunken charm all over the place. From brazenly but casually wooing Delta Goodrem's mum, to buying drinks for everyone and charging them to another band's room number, he was on fire. I thought, if this is a meltdown, then it looks pretty good to me. I wanted in.

We woke up the next afternoon next to each other in my hotel bed, with the worst hangovers either of us had had for a month. Okay, a week.

After that we were a couple. Seriously, it was like a platonic gay relationship. I loved the guy, but I didn't want to stick it in him. We just wanted to be around each other. And I think the people that were usually around him were tiring of all the drama, so I stepped in and was there for him at the right time.

We started going to football matches together. And at these times there wasn't a lot of talk about music and careers. It had a whole other context and setting when we went to the footy.

Tim's a North Melbourne supporter and I'm obviously a St Kilda guy. I would go to all sorts of North Melbourne games with Tim. North vs pretty much anyone. I just like going to watch football. Some people only want to go and see their team play but for me it doesn't matter whether it's St Kilda playing or not. I just like good footy. Actually I just like being AT the footy. Maybe it's the food.

We would also enjoy going for a kick together. It's a special little slice of bliss finding an empty park or oval on a mild autumn afternoon in Melbourne and kicking a football to one another. It's very therapeutic – it was good for us physically but it was especially good for our mental health. And we would talk, about everything. Kick, walk and talk. No subject too personal or private. Dudes like us need dudes like us.

It was many months before the inevitable idea of us playing together even came up (I mean we had played together quite a few times over the years, when I guested with You Am I) and looking back I think we avoided it for a while. But then we just couldn't help ourselves and a few pub gigs were booked. At its best it was like a comedy act with two acoustic guitars.

With boozy banter and beautiful ballads, we enjoyed entering each other's musical landscape.

Not long after that Tim was offered a very interesting gig. Every year the West Australian Symphony Orchestra does this special event where they get contemporary artists and do their songs in orchestral fashion. Tim was offered this but they wanted him to double-up with someone else. So he chose me! Thanks T.

Before we knew it we were both working with the West Australian Symphony Orchestra. Could this thing we were just starting be put in front of a 70-piece orchestra? Did they know what they were letting themselves in for? Did WE know what we were letting ourselves in for?

Six of Tim's songs and six of mine were chosen (by them) and orchestral scores were written to accompany them. At this stage we were both very much in the 'can't believe this is happening' frame of mind and pretty much just agreed with everything they wanted to do. We were astounded that our silly little four-chord rock songs were being used as templates for these enormously complex arrangements.

A month later we travelled to Perth to do publicity and hear the scores for the first time. We got there the night before and, of course, did some damage. So at ten o'clock in the morning we sat trembling with tears in our eyes from not only our own discomfort but the overwhelming experience of hearing our music played to us by a huge orchestra. It was breathtaking.

I have to admit when we actually started working with the WASO it was intimidating. To get in front of that many people, in the orchestra and in the audience, required some guts, believe me. We knuckled down and gave good rehearsal but when we were finally out there performing . . . it was out there.

One moment I will never forget was when I was about to sing one of my songs, the conductor steers the orchestra to my entry point and . . . I MISS MY CUE. The conductor and I share a quick glance and he turns back to the 70-piece orchestra and with a wave of his baton adds another four-bar intro. It was like turning the *Queen Mary* around on a dime.

'Wow,' I thought, he really saved my arse, and then I missed it again, another quick wave and . . . third time lucky, and we were away. Tim nailed his parts with no problems. No matter what else was going on he always gave good show at the gig.

After that the next thing we jumped into was the writing and recording of an album together. *My Better Half.* At first we would write separately. I would throw 'Half Of Nothing' at him and he would throw 'Any Old Time' at me. But then we wrote things like 'Everyone Hates You When You're Popular' and 'Cunnilingus' on the spot right there in the studio.

It was a T'N'T year and a good period for it because neither of us was overloaded with commitments with our other bands, so we embarked on a tour of Europe and America. If you ever want to test a friendship or a relationship, go on a long tour together.

Tim's a sensitive soul and I can be an insensitive oaf sometimes. More than once I hurt Tim's feelings without realising what I'd done. I never meant to, I'm just an idiot. His mood swings can be difficult to ride. After that tour we cooled off a bit and went our separate ways. We still see each other regularly but have been a little wary of working with each other again. But we will; it's inevitable. He's one of my all-time favourite musicians and one of the few true rock stars that this country has produced. Love ya, T.

MY BETTER HALF

T'N'T / 2006

Shane O'Mara's backyard garden shed studio was perfect
for Tim Rogers and I to scratch together this interesting
little album. It ain't perfect by a long shot but it has
some wonderful things on it. 'Cunnilingus' for one.
Tim's 'Dinosaurs' is one of the most beautifully vulnerable
songs ever recorded by anyone ever. It kills me.

RECORD LABEL: *Liberation*
CORE BAND MEMBERS: *Tex Perkins (vocals/guitar), Tim Rogers (vocals/guitar),
Shane Walsh (double bass), Shane O'Mara (guitar).*

THE APE - THE BAND

I'm into apes in any shape or form so I guess it was only a matter of time before I put together a band called The Ape.

The Ape came about as a vehicle for a lot of material that I had that I'd found no other place to use. It was stuff that I had hanging around that definitely wasn't Dark Horses material. It wasn't quite The Cruel Sea and it wasn't quite The Beasts Of Bourbon.

In some ways the genesis for this project goes back quite some way, and perhaps even earlier than I sometimes realise. It was probably in the middle of doing some working with Tex, Don & Charlie and The Dark Horses, bands whose music leads me into a variety of emotional areas.

I think sometimes I just need to make music for me that no one will ever hear – or at least when I'm coming up with it I'm thinking that it won't ever go out anywhere. That's fun for me. I really believe that not everything needs to be put out there for people to hear, but I guess I'm not alone in thinking that. There's probably a large chunk of my music some people wish I HAD just kept to myself.

I have lots of stuff – LOADS OF STUFF – that no one will ever hear. It's part of me just keeping my craft together, staying engaged with the fundamentals of putting music together.

There was a long period when I relied on James Cruickshank for demoing because he had a little studio set up. But then I moved to using a laptop and the Garage Band programme which I guess I've been using for about a decade now. That enabled me to always be dabbling in things and putting ideas down when they came to me, often just for the hell of it.

I had some drum loops that I played some riffs over and I built up four or five things that I made up and put down very quickly. It was exciting so I kept returning to it, and seemed to be edging towards something, but it never had a home or a context. I had no idea where I was going with it but I knew it didn't really fit any of my existing bands.

I saw this music as completely separate to what I was trying to do with everything else and I actually had this idea of creating an identity. Getting a bunch of cute 15-year-olds together and pretending they made this music together – and fool Triple J into playing it. It was a fantasy but I still hold on to that fantasy – to create something and not have me as the visual identity out there selling it. A Milli Vanilli sort of thing. I still might. But maybe you'll never know . . .

And that music eventually became The Ape. I hadn't played music with riffs and grooves for quite awhile. No opportunity to play it with anyone had presented itself, and it wasn't quite something I could put to The Beasts Of Bourbon. It wasn't dark enough for the Beasts but it was too heavy for The Cruel Sea. But over a couple of years of tinkering with these pieces of music and ideas I sort of built them in to songs and then I started to feel okay about a few people hearing them and when they did they said that they really liked them. So I started to believe they were telling me the truth.

Around the time when my last contracted solo record had been due, I decided to play the record company game and ask them what they wanted and engage with them and do demos and all that bullshit. I actually did demo some of those

The Ape, 2016.

songs for what I thought might be my next record. Believe it or not but I'd never done that before – we always just delivered whatever album it was to the record company, complete.

I demoed them with Kram of the band Spiderbait (who was great to work with) and then played them to the A&R man at the record company. That's when he decided that maybe a covers album might be good and we ended up doing the

Ladyboyz album. So that sort of knocked my confidence in those songs for awhile. You can imagine how it felt – you demo all these new songs that you think are pretty good and a guy at a record company listens to them and suggests you make a record of other people's songs. It's demoralising. But I knew the songs were good despite what this record company dick thought.

So the songs sat on the reject pile and more years went by and then I think I was at a stage where for some reason I wanted to do something and certain musicians weren't available as they were doing other things. I know Murray and Charlie were busy.

That made me realise that at times I've become just a little bit reliant on a comparatively small group of people to get something happening, and that if they're involved in other things I'm sort of stymied until their time frees up.

At this point I decided that I'd put together a new rock band and I'd call it The Ape. I could get people who were easy – and by that I mean easy to be with, easy to play with and fun to be around. The music wouldn't be introspective and it wouldn't be difficult. It would be rock music with grooves, riffs and melodies.

I immediately turned to Raul Sanchez, who I knew from Magic Dirt, for guitar and my go-to drummer, Gus Agars. I thought we needed a keyboard player – a utility musician who could play a lot of different things. We were looking for someone like that for awhile before I thought, *What a minute, I wrote those piano parts – we don't need a piano player to play piano parts that I wrote.* So when Pat Bourke agreed to play bass AND piano the line-up was complete. (Pat had never played piano before either.)

A few other people contributed to the album – Dan Luscombe, Mike Noga, and even Bob Murphy is in there doing vocals on 'Man On A Mission'. Is he the only captain of an AFL Premiership team on a rock record? Probably.

In some ways The Ape record is the most 'me' album that I've ever made. It's one project where I don't feel like I need to adopt a persona. The Dark Horses music is often introspective and melancholic, due to the fact that I write with Murray Paterson. His music is often dark and sweet so I follow that muse. The Beasts' music is dark and ugly so that leads me to those places. The Ape's music is heavy but it has a grin rather than a scowl. After all, apes just want to have fun. Tellingly, it's the only record I've done where I'm credited as Greg Perkins on the back cover – and not Tex.

The Ape is a great blend of what I love doing. It's got the sense of fun that can be found in The Cruel Sea and then there's bits of the Beasts heaviness about it but it's not as nihilistic. It's certainly heavy and it's very much a rock'n'roll record but I didn't need to turn into THAT GUY – which is maybe why I decided to use my real name on it.

With The Ape I can enjoy myself when I'm inside the songs. They have a power to them but also a humour. It strikes the right balance. Even though when I wrote all those songs I wrote them as something that wasn't really for me. I wrote them as an exercise in writing music and at the time I couldn't imagine myself actually playing them live. Partly, I guess, because I was using drum loops and had played everything myself. I wanted to do something I didn't usually do. It just came out very quickly without thought, context or analysis. I had no framework or a vision of where it was going to go.

So there's probably a lot more of me in there than even I realise. Any psychiatrist will tell you that this is where a lot of the truth will slip out – when you're doing something that you don't expect anyone else will hear.

As I said, I formed The Ape at a time when people I usually worked with were unavailable. I love The Ape, but lately it's getting harder to get everyone together. Gus and Pat have gigs with younger and more successful artists who can give them a smoother ride than I can. The age of The Ape may have already passed . . . Time for a new band.

THE APE

THE APE / 2013

One of my favourites to record and to listen to. My kids like this one – a 10-song rock'n'roll album with a grin, rather than a smirk or a scowl. Simplicity is the crucial element. It's made from songs I'd been accumulating over the last six years that never quite fit with any of my usual collaborators, although at various stages I thought to try some of them with The Cruel Sea and the Beasts. Some of them were part of the demos the A&R guy at Universal rejected that led to The Ladyboyz. I enjoyed playing heavy rock' n'roll music without having to channel some sleazebag or a homicidal maniac. This music was heavy, wild and loud, but fun. Raul Sanchez, who I'd known for many years by then, was the first I thought of to play guitar alongside me, Pat Bourke on bass, and of course, Gus Agars on drums. I love The Ape.

RECORD LABEL: *Bang! Records*
CORE BAND MEMBERS: *Greg Perkins (vocals/guitar), Raul Sanchez (guitar), Gus Agars (drums/vocals), Pat Bourke (bass/piano).*

SAVE THE PALAIS

I'd never aspired to be involved in politics.

The very idea of getting involved in that sort of thing seemed ridiculous, and not very much fun anyway. But sometimes somebody has just got to stand up and do something. The Palais Theatre campaign: my very successful manipulation of the political process in 2014.

The Palais Theatre is a state-owned, heritage-listed, but completely rundown art deco 3000 seat theatre near the beach in St Kilda. Although hosting thousands of local and international acts for more than 70 years, in 2014 it hadn't had any sort of standard maintenance for decades and was becoming increasingly dilapidated. It was being constantly used, but seemingly run into ground. There was a group of people who had been lobbying successive state governments saying that it

314

is the largest seated theatre venue in Australia, and if they let it deteriorate any further it wouldn't be able to be used at all. The argument was that the government owned it so they should cough up and get the restoration done.

But no one would do anything. It was really strange that it was such a non-issue with all these politicians. I mean, just look at the basics. If you have 3000 people going to see a show at the Palais before and after the show, they're all in the cafes, bars and restaurants around St Kilda spending money. Along with Luna Park, it's basically the nucleus of the local economy. You take the Palais out of the local St Kilda area and it's a very different outlook. Physically, culturally and economically.

But putting all that to one side, I basically just love the building. It's a huge deco thing with towers and turrets. It's beautifully monolithic and I've always loved it. I loved it way before I ever performed there. I loved it before I even went through the front doors. My love of the Palais is nothing about having great memories of gigs I played or anything like that. It's just a great love of its physicality and an appreciation of its history and of what it means to St Kilda.

Anyway, this group was lobbying the state government for many many years with no success. But in 2014 there was a campaign with a guy called Serge Thomann behind it. He was getting people involved and running this campaign called 'I LOVE MY PALAIS'. He was approaching actors, writers, musicians – anyone with some sort of a profile – and the idea was that you just had a photo of yourself taken with the I LOVE MY PALAIS sign in your hands.

The Rolling Stones played four nights in a row there back in 1964, and when they toured again in 2014 Mick Jagger made special mention of the building, urging the state government to wake up to its responsibilities. Even this made no difference.

Serge approached me and of course I said that I was happy to help in whatever way I could; I said that it was important and I'd do 'whatever it takes'. Saying the words 'whatever it takes' was a little bit of a flippant cliché, but I did say it. So Serge grabbed me from time to time during the campaign, usually to do any interview about the Palais.

Then he called me one day and said, 'Tex, I must see you, I have an idea.' I was on my way to a rehearsal so I said I could meet him for 10 minutes. We dashed into a cafe and he says, 'Tex, you will run as an independent in the state election.'

'This guy's lost it,' I thought.

The Palais is in a marginal seat, the electorate of Albert Park, and Martin Foley, the ALP guy, had a majority of less than one per cent. Serge's idea was that I would run in the election with just one policy – to save the Palais. The margin in the electorate was so slim that any vote changes – anything that took votes away from one candidate and to another – could really make a difference. I thought he was insane. But the more I thought about it, the more it sounded like mischief. And you know how I love mischief.

Okay, so now I'm running as a candidate in an election, with just one policy. But in the context of the votes in that area it's a significant one and one that gets lots of media exposure. I was on the front page of *The Age* when it was announced that I was running and immediately the phone started ringing.

The thinking was that we expected Foley to win, and we wanted him to win as he was the incumbent Labor guy. I met with the Liberals but they weren't prepared to offer any deal beyond saying that they 'liked' the Palais. (Phew.) The Greens were right behind me but they weren't expected to win. So basically I had to make a deal with Foley.

Not only was I dealing with Martin but also his supporters. Labor people came out hard against me. One particular columnist launched a series of very ugly attacks not only on me, but the Palais itself and St Kilda in general. 'Fuck the Palais, let it save itself,' said she. 'Who goes to St Kilda anyway? Yeah sure it was cool in the '90s but now it's an uncool junkie sinkhole.'

While she flapped and squawked about 'hidden motives', and that I 'didn't belong on the ballot', she missed the whole point of the exercise: I didn't want votes, I wanted to make some noise and make a deal. While she tried to connect 'punk rock' with the Palais (what the?) and somehow make this about the glory days of the '90s, the deal was being done. She and her online congratulators, missing the point once again, compared me to Peter Garrett and Bono. I gotta admit that hurt. Meanwhile the deal was done, but I had to keep quiet until Labor made its policy announcement.

The other thing I noticed during that time was Labor's growing hatred towards the Greens and Independents. If yer not with us, yer against us! It's sad. It's like they resent anyone more Left than them. The Greens have stolen their soul, as

Labor try to stay as close to the centre as possible, gradually and inevitably becoming irrelevant. Still smarting from the fallout over Gillard's coalition with the Greens, Labor believes the voters turned on them because of the policies they were forced into. But really, it was just that Gillard was a terrible saleswoman and Rudd is a narcissistic nutjob.

Anyway, Martin wanted to take on my policy and that made me (happily) redundant. I agreed to endorse him and give him my preferences. And that's what happened. He personally wanted to save the Palais anyway but he didn't have the leverage to go back to his party and tell them that they needed to put some funding into its restoration. Me saying I was running gave him that leverage as they couldn't risk me giving my preferences to someone else, particularly the Liberals – which of course I didn't want to do. But this pressure made them realise that there was a very real possibility that he could lose his seat, so the whole thing worked perfectly. Anyway, it was just the right thing to do, and he's a good man.

Labor announced a thirteen-million-dollar contribution to its restoration, I endorsed Foley and the policy and then from that point on I told people not to vote for me. I kept campaigning right up until the election telling people NOT to vote for me and they'd say, 'What a unique, refreshing approach, I'm voting for you.' It was a total Catch-22. For a little while I was sweating with the idea that I might actually win, and that would've been the worst result of all.

I don't think I ever actually said the words 'Vote For Me', but in the end about 1300 people did. And that was the sort of margin that could have made a difference if my preferences went elsewhere.

Something that nobody knew at the time was that I had the backing of the CFMEU. Dave Noonan, the head of the union, is an old friend of The Beasts Of Bourbon. He and I had a meeting during the election campaign. We threw around a few ideas including a union green ban if it got to the demolition stage. It was good to have his support. He's a good man and far from the thug union boss the conservative filth try to portray him as. Although being an old friend of The Beasts Of Bourbon wouldn't necessarily help his reputation.

I have to say, I bluffed my way through this whole thing. At the start I had no idea, but I learned quick. The mental pressure I was under for those four weeks was immense, and I was glad when it was over.

In the end Foley and the Labor party won and today the Palais is in good nick and continues to function. Me? I voted for the Greens and went back to doing whatever I was doing before.

OTHER STUFF

There have been many one-off collaborations, coalitions and collisions over the years. So many I will probably forget to mention a few but what I definitely remember is recording a version of Kev Carmody's 'Darkside' for the *Cannot Buy My Soul* tribute album and show put together by Paul Kelly. A song Kev wrote with a group of street kids from the notorious Logan city, south of Brisbane, it's a spoken word street poetry docudrama that transports me to that world with startling efficiency.

In 2007 I was asked to contribute a song to the album *No Woman's Man* and to choose a song normally associated with a woman. 'I Am Woman' by Helen Reddy was the first and only song that jumped into my head. My ragged version apparently offended some people. Other people were offended by the very fact I chose that particular song. (A feminist anthem can't be sung by a dude? For fuck's sake.) Looking back they should consider themselves lucky I didn't go for 'Natural Woman' by Aretha Franklin.

Paul Mac approached me about singing a song on his album. I didn't know much about Paul but I remember he was in a noisy electronic band in the '80s called Smash Mac Mac. I said, 'Give me a CD and I'll give the demo a listen.' The song was 'Heat Seeking Pleasure Machine', a sleazy techno grinder of a thing. I thought it was hilarious and it kicked arse. It felt like it should be played in a leather club, but this was way too heavy for those boys; anyway I think they'd rather fist-fuck to Kylie Minogue

Corroboration was an album of various black and white

Australian artists collaborating. The Cruel Sea teamed up with hip hop group Native Rhyme, with Magoo producing and Martin Lee, ex of Regurgitator, programming the drum machine. The song 'Together' was written and recorded in a day and is remarkable. The final touch is the appearance of Kev Carmody, who happened to be visiting me at the time, at the end of the track. Kev lends his considerable skills as a poet but also as a vocal performer. His very presence gives this track a sense of authenticity.

A few years ago I received an email from a band called Cookin on 3 Burners. Attached to the email was the demo of a song called 'Flat on my back' and an invitation to record the vocal for the track. It was a stripped-back funk track with plenty of chicken in its strut, so I immediately agreed.

Jake, Ivan and Dan are a 'crack unit' as they say. They're a really great instrumental band and I've had the pleasure of playing with them live many times now. Sometimes it reminds me of another instrumental band I played with many moons ago . . .

My dear friend, actor and musician, Justine Clarke is the queen of ABC television's kids' show *Play School*. Her album *I Like To Sing* revolutionised kids' music, as it was attractive to children but could be enjoyed by parents as well (unlike some other 'artists' who will remain nameless). The king to her queen of *Play School* is/was Rhys Muldoon. I've known Rhys for many years, and was delighted when he asked me to help out with his album of music for kids. Produced by Kram, *I'm Not Singing* is the counter balance to Justine's *I Like To Sing*. Possessing lots of great tunes that are tolerable to adults, it's wilder, edgier and harder-rocking than kids' music usually is. But personally, I would've only put one song about poo on the album.

CAREER DIVERSITY BLUES

There was always going to be a price to pay for a career as musically all over the place as mine was.

It definitely wasn't planned that way. I know audiences get confused, others have felt betrayed. I can understand. If you have a certain audience and they've gotten used to, for instance, hard rock'n'rolling from me and then I do something SENSITIVE and ACOUSTIC they feel betrayed, and vice versa. They might see me with a funk band one time, and next time they see me it's with a country band.

It drives some people crazy, but hey . . .

You win some, you lose some.

On reflection I wouldn't have really wanted it any other way. I'm not sure I'd have wanted to do just The Beasts Of Bourbon for the past 30 years. I wouldn't be here.

All my life, as a kid and as an adult, I've always enjoyed doing different things. That philosophy and the approach to the way I work really solidified in the Black Eye period where I made a band up, did a gig and then a week later I put together a completely different thing to do one show or a few. I guess I got used to being in five different bands at once.

In the early '90s I was seriously playing in The Beasts Of Bourbon and The Cruel Sea, touring at home and abroad, and recording with both bands. Then Tex, Don & Charlie came along and I fit those shows into the mix too. That was the way I worked – and it's still the way I work. I act on what is around and presenting itself and that triggers my ability and desire to work. It's simply a case of my seeing opportunities and saying 'THAT LOOKS LIKE FUN – I'LL DO IT!'

It's why I've been able to look after my family and have a life I love without having to go back to sweeping floors or selling foam mattresses to supplement a music career.

There's not a lot of other Australian musicians from the early 1980s who are still out there doing it consistently like I am. There's a lot who had a good couple of years – maybe a good decade – and then they had to get a 'real job'. I've been at it for over three-and-a-half decades without having to have a day job in the traditional sense. Like all working musicians, it can be feast followed by famine. Sometimes there's no money for a frighteningly long time. But I make it work. Music is my job. But it's not only my job. It's not only my career. It's my love. It's my obsession.

It's *what* I am and it's *why* I am.

The reality is that if you're in just one band AND you're successful you still only have maybe 10 years at it – if you're VERY lucky. That's 10 years of operating at the proper touring, recording and making money level. Even less the way music is today.

Tex, Don & Charlie, we only do every 12 years but it's *always there* and when those dozen years roll around again it's 'Hey, time to do another record', just like always.

Actually, between this TDC record and the last, I've worked with Tim Rogers, the West Australian Symphony Orchestra, the Sydney Youth Orchestra, made a Beasts record for Alberts, unleashed The Ladyboyz, made three Dark Horses albums, formed a new band, The Ape, released a country standards album, recorded and toured with funk soul specialists Cookin on 3 Burners, done hundreds of solo and duo gigs all round the world with Charlie Owen or Murray Paterson, done voiceovers for cartoons, ads and documentaries, worked with Doc Neeson, Justine Clarke, Chad Morgan, Jimmy Barnes, Ron Barassi, Lydia Lunch and Brian Cadd, sung 5000 Johnny Cash songs, scored several film soundtracks, worked in theatre, revived The Cruel Sea for what we now realise was a farewell tour and have lost count of how many times I've appeared on Rockwiz. It's a lot to figure out, but it's a lot of fun.

I do my damnedest to make everything I'm involved in work, but the two really successful projects I've been involved with, The Cruel Sea and *The Man In Black*, have made me feel trapped. Because if something is successful you are logically obliged to keep doing it, and doing it. Successful bands do long tours, successful theatre shows do long seasons. After a while it's difficult to feel engaged in what you're doing, and that can be dangerous, as you grapple with ways of battling the monotony. It's not just sharks that die if they stop moving.

I change things up constantly. So if, as they say, a change is as good as holiday, then I'm permanently on vacation.

Anyway, I kinda operate in my own alternate universe where I can sell out a 700-seat venue with The Ape in Adelaide and run into someone at the airport the next day who says, 'You're Tex Perkins aren't you? Do you still play music?' And that for me is perfect, getting the job done but flying under the radar.

As a wise man once said, 'There's a difference between scratching your arse and ripping it to shreds'. My arse was only a little itchy, but it's still itchy.

As I said before, I think I did all this back then so I had something to put in this fucking book. When you're old you gotta have a few crazy stories to tell about yourself.

The trick is remembering them.

OUTRO

Some of you might be wondering *why is there a book about THIS guy?*

I mean let's break it down to facts and stats.

I'm a white Australian male.

I'm a musician, primarily a singer.

I write songs, but I don't see myself as a songwriter. I'm a singer in need of something to sing.

My career equates to one number one album and six ARIA awards, and all totalled, probably a little over a million albums sold across 34 years and with more than 20 different bands. My biggest selling record was only about 250,000. These are not impressive figures, when compared to Barbra Streisand or U2 or even the Hoodoo Gurus.

I admit I didn't have much interest in my story myself. Not until I started telling it. That's when I realised it's not the big picture that's interesting, it's the little ones – all the fuck-ups that hurt at the time, but now are wonderful memories that make me laugh. (Most of them anyway.) And all those unique individuals I've met and all the wonderful stupid things we've done together.

It's also all the great music that has moved me over that time. Moved me, not only emotionally, but moved me along with my life. The songs that got me going, fuelled my imagination and taught me how to live. *Why to live.*

This book all started when I got an email from Stuart Coupe in April 2016.

It was titled 'Life and Projects'.

Hmmm, bit weird.

Haven't really had much to do with Stuart for a few years.

But he was always someone I respected and never had a problem with, so I not only opened the email, but I also read it!

These days Stuart is a writer, a weekly DJ on two Sydney independent radio stations, a father and a husband, and he pretends to be a football coach.

But when I first met him he was one half of record label Green Records, a band manager, journalist and sometime promoter.

So 'Life and Projects' could've meant anything.

'Would love to get together for a chat,' he wrote.

Hmmm, what are you up to Coupes?

I answered and agreed 'to have a chat'.

Anyway turns out he wants to write a book, about me!

Well, actually he wants me to write it, with him pushing me along.

Oh fuck.

Really?

Are you sure?

Yeah, says he's 'got a publisher and everything, actually they came to me with the idea'.

Hmmm, really?

No. Thanks anyway.

Those rock books (of which I've read a few) are usually about how much money they made, how many ladies they 'knew', how many drugs they took, and there's an avalanche of name-dropping along the way.

And yes, I have done all those things, but not in any great numbers that seemed worthy of a tell-all rock bio.

Somewhere along the line Stuart tried to assure me that this wouldn't be like that and that we could (together) take it in any direction I liked.

Still I was not totally convinced.

I mean what's the angle?

What's interesting?

What's the scoop Coupe?

The story of an awkward skinny kid from the northern suburbs of Brisbane who grows up to be in lots of bands with silly names, one of which sold a few albums a few years ago . . . back when people gave a shit.

Hmmmm. Nah. I don't think I need a thorough examination of my . . . what?

The advance is how much?

Really?

Do we have to split that?

No?

That's just for me?

Hmmm, well I suppose . . .

And then Stuart said the words that always get me.

'We'll have fun!'

And I was in.

Prick!

THANK YOUS AND ACKNOWLEDGEMENTS

From Tex

First of all, I'd like to acknowledge those we've loved who have gone before us. Bob Perkins, Shane Walsh, Peter Read, Speedy, Tony Carmona and James Cruickshank. Wish you were here.

I'd like to thank all my comrades over the years, but especially Brian Hooper, Tony Pola, Danny Rumour, Stuart Grey and Spencer Jones. Thanks for letting me tell everyone how much fun we had and how stupid we were.

Special thanks to Jules Normington and John Foy.

Eternal thanks to Iggy Pop.

I want to thank my best friend and partner, Kristyna, for giving me the time and space to write.

I'd like to thank Andrea for reading the thing and suggesting changes. Big thanks to my brother Rob for jogging my memory on a few of the details. Also thanks to Juan Mari Iturrarte for his relentless enthusiasm.

Thanks to Angus Fontaine for starting this whole process, and Georgia Douglas at Macmillan, you were great to work with. Thanks also to Ingrid Ohlsson and Alex Craig.

I'd like to thank Stuart Coupe for pushing me into this thing and telling me it would be fun. It was.

But really I'd like to thank everyone for all the adventures we've shared and giving me some meat to put in the sandwich. (I'm talking about this book.)

From Stuart

When this book was first mooted by Angus Fontaine, little did I realise what a long, occasionally fraught and frequently fun and illuminating year-and-a-half it would be.

Tex knocked on my door when he first arrived in Sydney in the early 1980s, and three-and-a-half decades later I still consider him a good buddy. At the beginning I promised him a fun time with this book, and for the majority of the time our working relationship has been exactly that. He's also maintained a consistent domination in our frequent stress-relieving table-tennis matches. So to Tex – thanks for the table tennis, candid chats and laughs.

Along the way I received valuable assistance from John Willsteed, Greg Manson, Murray Bennett, Patrick Emery, Robert Dunstan, John Foy and Rob Fadaely. Thank you all.

As the book progressed, Georgia Douglas at Pan Macmillan did an amazing job of pulling everything together. My favourite line: 'Stuart, we're working from five different versions of the manuscript – let's consolidate them into one, can we?' And a further big nod of gratitude to Heather Rose, who gets the award for Tough But Fair Diplomatic Negotiator (TBFDN).

Susan Lynch was along for the whole ride. She's my heart, soul, best friend and companion in all the adventures, crazy times and experiences that we embark on.

Thank you to everyone – and thank you again, Susan.

OK, as Tex says, 'That'll do.'

TOP TEN
ALBUMS
BY PERKO

1. THE AXEMAN'S JAZZ / THE BEASTS OF BOURBON

2. SAD BUT TRUE / TEX, DON & CHARLIE

3. WHERE THERE'S SMOKE / THE CRUEL SEA

4. DARK HORSES / TEX PERKINS

5. THE APE / THE APE

6. *BEAUTIFUL KATE* / TEX PERKINS, MURRAY PATERSON

7. ALL IS FORGIVEN / TEX, DON & CHARLIE

8. THREE LEGGED DOG / THE CRUEL SEA

9. TEX PERKINS AND THE BAND OF GOLD /
   TEX PERKINS AND THE BAND OF GOLD

10. YOU DONT KNOW LONELY / TEX, DON & CHARLIE

TEX'S PLAYLIST

To enhance your reading experience

'Born On A Bayou', Creedence Clearwater Revival

'I'm Eighteen', Alice Cooper

'I'm Branded', Link Wray

'Rock Island Line', Johnny Cash

'Runaway Boys', Stray Cats

'Garbageman', The Cramps

'Set It On Fire', The Scientists

'Feel The Pain', The Damned

'Nightclubbing', Iggy Pop

'She Said', Hasil Adkins

'Zoo Music Girl', The Birthday Party

'Nothing Grows In Texas', Sacred Cowboys

'Sex Beat', The Gun Club

'Crawfish', Elvis Presley

'Psychotic Reaction', The Count Five

'Double Talkin' Baby', Gene Vincent

'Planet Claire', The B52s

'Jump Sturdy', Dr John

'Warren Smith', Uranium Rock

'Dead Flowers', The Rolling Stones

'Swamp Witch', Jim Stafford

'Jolene', Dolly Parton

'Louie Louie', The Sonics

'Paralysed', Legendary Stardust Cowboy

'The Fatal Wedding', Chad Morgan

'All By Myself', Johnny Burnette

'Train Round The Bend', The Velvet Underground

'You're Driving Me Insane', The Missing Links

'I've Had It', Alex Chilton

'Hot Head', Captain Beefheart

'Jukebox Baby', Alan Vega

'The Man With The Harmonica', Ennio Morricone

'Mushroom', Can

'The Fish Needs A Bike', Blurt

'In Dark Trees', Brian Eno

'Pablo Picasso', Modern Lovers

'30 Seconds Over Tokyo', Pere Ubu

'Nova Feedback', Chrome

'Dead Men Walks', Jad Fair

'Lady Scarface', Lydia Lunch

'Ich Bin's', Einstürzende Neubauten

'Yellow Black And Rectangular', Negativland

'You'll See Glimpses', Ian Dury & The Blockheads

'Hello Skinny', The Residents

'You Know My Name (Look Up The Number)',
The Beatles

'Boogie Stop Shuffle', Charles Mingus

'Morbius' Study', Louis and Bebe Barron

'Cruenta Voluptas', Non

'This Bloke Came Up To Me', Derek and Clive

'Performance', Jack Nitzsche

'Contort Yourself', James Chance and the Contortions

'Thing With A Hook', Half Japanese

'What Do You Know About Music, You're Not A
Lawyer', John Lurie

'Shore Leave', Tom Waits

'Loser', Beck

'Gimme Back My Wig', Hound Dog Taylor

'Sophisticated Cissy', The Meters

'Crazy Baldhead', Bob Marley

'Bron-Yr-Aur', Led Zeppelin

'The Partisan', Leonard Cohen

'Big Eyed Beans From Venus', Captain Beefheart

'Hush Hush', Jimmy Reed

'Welcome To The Terrordome', Public Enemy

'Little Doll', The Stooges

'Moonlight Mile', The Rolling Stones

'Fire And Brimstone', Link Wray

'Everything Is Free', Gillian Welch

'Witchy Woman', The Eagles

'The Chain', Fleetwood Mac

'Don't Want To Know', John Martyn

'Journey In Satchidananda', Alice Coltrane

'They Say I'm Different', Betty Davis

'Cold Gin', Kiss

'Childhood's End', Pink Floyd

'One Flew Over The Cuckoo's Nest', Jack Nitzsche

'Crazy Mama', JJ Cale

'Fair Play', Van Morrison

'Scorpio's View', Lalo Schifrin

'Friday's Child', Nancy Sinatra

'Bring Me My Shotgun', Lightnin' Hopkins

'Ramblin' Man', Hank Williams

'Don't Let It Bring You Down', Neil Young

'Waiting Around To Die', Townes Van Zandt

'Don't Let Me Be Misunderstood', Nina Simone

'High Sheriff Of Calhoun Parrish', Tony Joe White

'Werewolves Of London', Warren Zevon

'A Gift', Lou Reed

'Mr Tambourine Man', William Shatner

'Float On', The Floaters

'AAXXX', Peaches

'The Boys', The Necks

'One And One', Miles Davis

'I've Been Trying', DJ Shadow

'I Feel Love', Donna Summer

'Long Train Runnin'', The Doobie Brothers

'I'll Bet You', Funkadelic

'Hot Pants Road', The JB's

'I Ain't Superstitious', Howlin' Wolf

'I've Seen That Movie Too', Elton John

'Planet Of The Apes (Main Theme)', Jerry Goldsmith

'It's No Game', David Bowie

'Ho Renomo', Cluster & Eno

'Puff The Magic Dragon', The Seekers

'Cristo Rendentor', Donald Byrd

'Fixin' To Die Blues', Bukka White

'Thirteen', Johnny Cash

'I'm A Fool To Want You', Bob Dylan

'Goodbye', Steve Earle